Memory Quilts

IN THE MAKING

Compiled and edited by
Rhonda Richards

Oxmoor
House®

Memory Quilts IN THE MAKING

from the *For the Love of Quilting* series
©1999 by Oxmoor House, Inc.
Book Division of Southern Progress Corporation
P.O. Box 2262, Birmingham, Alabama 35201-2262

Published by Oxmoor House, Inc.

Library of Congress Catalog Card Number: 99-71765
Hardcover ISBN: 0-8487-1871-2
Softcover ISBN: 0-8487-1872-0
Printed in the United States of America
Sixteenth Printing 2008

Editor-in-Chief: Nancy Fitzpatrick Wyatt
Senior Crafts Editor: Susan Ramey Cleveland
Senior Editor, Copy and Homes: Olivia Kindig Wells
Art Director: James Boone

Memory Quilts IN THE MAKING

Editor: Rhonda Richards
Contributing Technical Writer: Laura Morris Edwards
Contributing Copy Editor: Susan Smith Cheatham
Editorial Assistant: Lauren Caswell Brooks
Associate Art Director: Cynthia R. Cooper
Contributing Designer: Rita Yerby
Illustrator: Kelly Davis
Senior Photographer: John O'Hagan
Contributing Photographer: Keith Harrelson
Photo Stylist: Linda Baltzell Wright
Contributing Photo Stylist: Melanie Clark
Director, Production and Distribution: Phillip Lee
Associate Production Manager: Theresa L. Beste
Production Assistant: Faye Porter Bonner

To order additional publications, call 1-800-765-6400.

For more books to enrich your life, visit
oxmoorhouse.com

From the Editor

Friendship quilts represent love. Whenever I come across an antique signature quilt, I wonder who made it and for what occasion. I touch the embroidered signatures and wonder if any of the participants are still with us.

A signature quilt inspires me to organize one myself to remind me of the people who love me and to commemorate special milestones in my life. It gratifies me that I can use my quilting skills to make something special for someone I love.

To me, there is nothing more comforting than snuggling up in a memory quilt with a cat in my lap and a cup of hot chocolate in my hand. I hope that these quilts will inspire you. Within these pages, you'll find everything from antique signature quilts to modern photo transfer and T-shirt quilts.

How to Use This Book

We've tried to make this book as user friendly as possible. We give full instructions for the quilts so that you can make them, beginning to end, yourself, complete with color diagrams, photos, and how-to photography for techniques you might not have tried yet. We did this so that if your circle of friends and family does not include any quilters, you can still make a friendship quilt. Simply give them a block or a fabric piece to sign, and then follow the instructions to make the entire quilt.

On the other hand, you may be part of a quilting guild that makes friendship blocks for incoming members or outgoing presidents. I know from experience that one of the most challenging tasks (once the pattern is chosen) is to figure the cutting and the yardage required just to make one block. Then there is always the confusion about what "finished size" means.

Members ask, "Is my block supposed to measure 8" or 8½"?"

To make this task easier, you'll find special instructions called "Block by Block" for signature quilts. This section will give complete yardage, cutting, and instructions for making just one block. We even tell you what size the block should measure once you're done! Use these instructions when you are having other people make a single block—if you are making the entire quilt yourself, you won't need this section.

Chapters in This Book

We've grouped the quilts by technique to help you quickly find the design you're looking for.

SIGNATURE QUILTS

Quilts featured in this section are ideal for showcasing signatures. In some cases, we found quilts using the same block but set entirely differently. Signature quilts can have either names written in permanent, fabric-safe ink, or they can be covered with embroidery stitches. They may also feature sayings, sentiments, or stamped images.

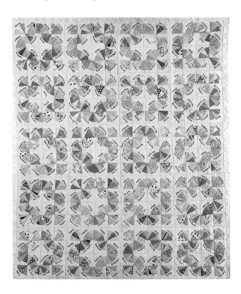

FOND MEMORIES

Every quilt has a story, and Fond Memories includes quilts whose stories touched our hearts. Some are happy and some are sad, but each has special meaning.

From the Editor

HANDKERCHIEF AND MEMORABILIA QUILTS

I love going to antique shops and flea markets. As a result, I have many jars of old buttons and drawers full of vintage linens. I've often wondered what I can do to get the most enjoyment from them.

The quilts in this section show you how to get those items out of hiding and to showcase them in a stunning quilt. You'll find examples of wall hangings, bed quilts, and even garments that make beautiful use of these treasures.

T-SHIRT QUILTS

I like to think of T-shirt quilts as the utility quilts of our age. Instead of viewing them as heirlooms, consider them more as scrapbooks—a record of a person's interests and experiences translated into fabric.

If you or a loved one can't bear to throw away old T-shirts that have outlived their use but still have high sentimental value, try making a T-shirt quilt. You will have recycled usable material and created a personal memento that can wrap its recipient in love.

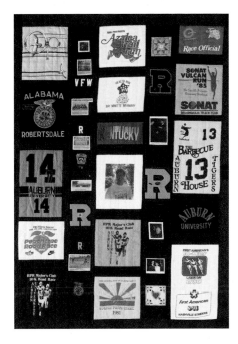

PHOTO TRANSFER QUILTS

One of the hottest trends in the last few years is photo transfer. There are many techniques available, but you'll find simple instructions for doing it yourself on page 135. After this how-to section, you'll find five quilts for inspiration. Some are block style, some are freeform, and some are simply joined by sashing strips to fit as many photos as possible. Let these quilts inspire you to make your own photo transfer quilt in *your* style.

IN THE SEWING ROOM

You'll find a workshop of quilting techniques in this section. These are techniques you can apply to almost any quilt in the book (you'll find specific techniques, like photo transfer, with the appropriate quilts).

In addition to covering the basics, we've updated the workshop to include tips for writing on fabric, working with rubber stamps, and using your computer to make quilt blocks and labels.

Let's Quilt!

Throughout the book, you'll find poems, quotes, and passages. Some are thousands of years old, and some were written by quilt-makers featured in this book. If you find one special to you, include it in your quilt label or in a signature block.

Whether the quilt is for yourself, a family member, or a friend, you are creating a memory that will be cherished.

Rhonda Richards

Contents

Signature Quilts

Fond Memories

Handkerchief and Memorabilia Quilts

T-Shirt Quilts

Photo Transfer Quilts

In the Sewing Room

Fan Quilt

Gwen Cox, of Birmingham, Alabama, purchased this quilt for $3.50 at a Salvation Army Thrift Store in 1985. When she saw several names of Birmingham businesses on the quilt, she realized it was made locally and immediately began research-ing its origin. See page 11 for the story.

Fan Quilt

Finished Size: 68" x 84"
Blocks: 20 (16") Baby Bunting
Blocks [320 (4") Fan Units]

Materials

5 yards light yellow for blocks
5 yards total assorted 1930s
   prints for blocks
1 yard white for border (2½
   yards for unpieced borders)
5 yards muslin for backing
Twin-size batting

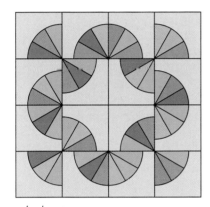

Block Diagram

Cutting

Measurements include ¼" seam
allowances. Cut fabric selvage to
selvage unless otherwise noted.

From light yellow, cut:
- 36 (4½"-wide) strips. Cut strips
  into 320 (4½") squares.

From assorted 1930s prints, cut:
- 960 As.

From white, cut:
- 8 (2½"-wide) strips. Piece to
  make 2 (2½" x 64½") top and
  bottom border strips and 2
  (2½" x 84½") side border
  strips. If you prefer unpieced
  borders, cut 4 (2½"-wide)
  lengthwise strips from alternate
  yardage and trim to size.

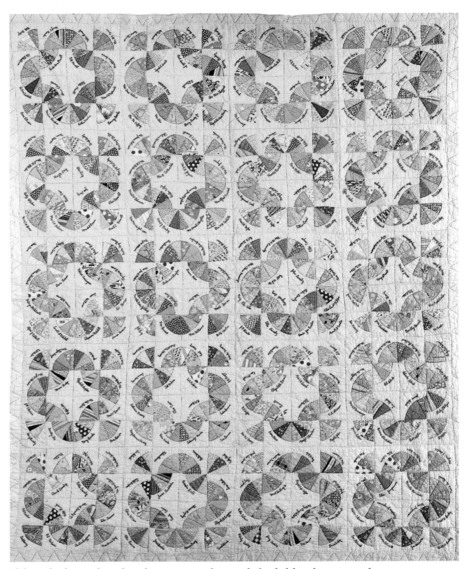

Although the embroidered names on this quilt look like they were done on a modern, computerized sewing machine, they were actually done in the 1930s by a quilter who was very skillful in using a satin-stitch feature on her machine.

Block Assembly

1. Join 3 As to make 1 fan.
2. Appliqué fan to 4½" yellow
square as shown in *Block Assembly
Diagram*. Trim fabric behind fan,
leaving ¼" seam allowance. Make
16 Fan units.
3. Lay out units as shown in *Block
Assembly Diagram*. Join to make 1
Baby Bunting block (*Block
Diagram*).
4. Make 20 Baby Bunting blocks.

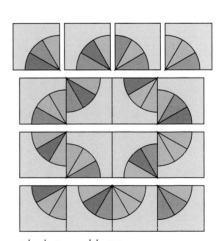

Block Assembly Diagram

Quilt Assembly

1. Arrange blocks in 5 horizontal rows of 4 blocks each. Join into rows; join rows to complete center.
2. Measure to ensure that borders will fit. Join 2 (2½" x 64½") borders to top and bottom of quilt. Add 2 (2½" x 84½") borders to quilt sides.

Quilting and Finishing

1. Divide backing fabric into 2 (2½-yard) lengths. Join along long sides to make backing.
2. Layer backing, batting, and quilt top; baste. Quilt as desired. Quilt shown was quilted in-the-ditch, with Vs in border.
3. Trim batting even with quilt top. Trim backing to 2" around all sides of quilt.
4. Fold backing in half toward quilt and press. Fold again to front and slipstitch in place to make ½"-wide binding. Miter corners.

Fan Quilt
BLOCK BY BLOCK

*Instructions for 1 (4")
Fan Signature Block*

MATERIALS
1 (4½") light yellow square
3 As in assorted 1930s prints

BLOCK ASSEMBLY
1. Join 3 As to make 1 fan.
2. Appliqué fan to 4½" yellow square. Trim fabric behind fan, leaving ¼" seam allowance. Block should measure 4½". Sign block.

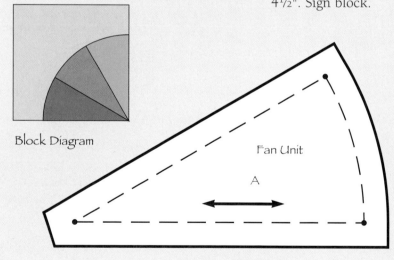

Block Diagram

Fan Unit

A

A friend loves at all times.

—*Proverbs 17:17 (NIV)*

STORY OF THE FAN QUILT

When Gwen Cox realized that the antique quilt she'd purchased had the names of several old Birmingham businesses, she resolved to find out the history behind this lost treasure.

"I began by cataloging all the names on the quilt so I'd have a handy list," says Gwen. "I tried to locate people on the list, but they were either deceased or didn't remember anything about the quilt."

Several years later, Gwen displayed the quilt in a local quilt show. Dr. Tom Caldwell, a retired Birmingham pediatrician, saw the quilt and happened to know someone whose name appeared on a block.

Once Gwen reached this person, she learned that the quilt was made in the 1930s by a group of women at a Methodist church in East Lake, a suburb of Birmingham. To raise funds for charity, they charged a dime for the privilege of having names put on a block. Then, upon its completion, the quilt was raffled to raise even more money. No one knows how much money it brought in, and the church no longer exists.

"What I found most intriguing," says Gwen, "was that one woman embroidered all the names on the blocks. They look like they were done on a computerized sewing machine, but she was just that skillful with her machine satin stitch."

Sister's Choice

Susan Cleveland received Sister's Choice friendship blocks from members of the Birmingham Quilters' Guild as the 1995–96 outgoing president. "I chose Sister's Choice because I like the pattern, and because I think of our guild members as my sisters and brothers," says Susan. She requested that the blocks be pieced in pastel colors to give the quilt a soft, old-fashioned look. Hand-quilted by Roxie Elliott.

Sister's Choice

Finished Size: 86" x 86"
Blocks: 49 (10") Sister's Choice
Blocks

Materials

1 yard total scraps dark prints for
blocks
2¾ yards total scraps medium
prints for blocks and sashing
squares
2½ yards total scraps light prints
for blocks
3¾ yards muslin for signature
area, sashing, and binding
7½ yards muslin for backing
Queen-size batting

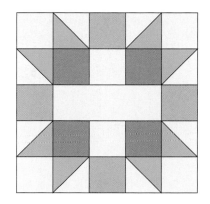

Block Diagram

By virtue of its name alone, Sister's Choice lends itself well to guild quilts, bee quilts, and church quilts. Or collect family signatures as a special gift for a beloved sister.

Cutting

Measurements include ¼" seam
allowances. Cut fabric selvage to
selvage unless otherwise noted.

From dark prints, cut:
• 49 sets of 4 (2½") squares (A).

From medium prints, cut:
• 64 assorted 2½" sashing squares.
• 49 sets of 4 (2½") squares for
medium #2 (A).
• 49 sets of 4 (2⅞") squares. Cut
squares in half diagonally to
make 8 medium #1 half-square
triangles (C).

From light prints, cut:
• 49 sets of:
  • 4 (2½") squares (A).
  • 4 (2⅞") squares. Cut squares
  in half diagonally to make 8
  half-square triangles (C).

From muslin, cut:
• 28 (2½"-wide) strips. Cut strips
into 112 (2½" x 10½") rectangles for sashing strips.
• 14 (2½"-wide) strips. Cut strips
into 98 (2½") squares A and 49
(2½" x 6½") rectangles B.
• 9 (2¼"-wide) strips for binding.

Block Assembly

1. Join 4 dark As, 2 muslin As, and
1 muslin B as shown in *Diagram 1*
to make center section.
2. Join 1 light C and 1 medium #1
C as shown in *Diagram 2* to make
1 half-square triangle unit. Make 8
C half-square triangle units.
3. Join 1 C unit to each side of 1
medium #2 A square as shown in
Diagram 3. Make 4 A/C strips.
4. Join 1 light A square to each end
of 1 A/C strip as shown in *Diagram
4* to make top strip. Repeat to
make bottom strip.
5. Join 1 A/C strip to each side of
center section as shown in *Block
Assembly Diagram*.

Sister's Choice

6. Join 1 top strip and 1 bottom strip to block as shown to complete (*Block Diagram*).

7. Make 49 Sister's Choice blocks.

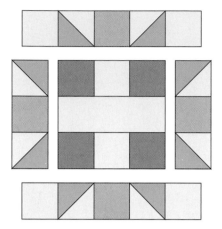

Block Assembly Diagram

Quilt Assembly

1. Referring to *Sashing Row Assembly Diagram*, alternate 7 sashing strips and 8 sashing squares. Join into a row. Make 8 sashing rows.

2. Referring to *Block Row Assembly Diagram*, alternate 7 blocks and 8 sashing strips. Join into a row. Make 7 block rows.

3. Referring to photo, alternate sashing rows and block rows. Join rows to complete quilt.

Quilting and Finishing

1. Divide backing fabric into 3 (2½-yard) lengths. Cut 1 piece in half lengthwise. Sew 1 narrow panel between wide panels. Press seam allowances toward narrow panel. Seams will run horizontally; remaining narrow panel is extra.

2. Layer backing, batting, and quilt top; baste. Quilt as desired. Quilt shown was outline-quilted.

3. Join 2¼"-wide muslin strips into 1 continuous piece for straight-grain French-fold binding. Add binding to quilt.

> *We all live in suspense, from day to day, from hour to hour; in other words, we are the hero of our own story.*
>
> —Mary McCarthy
> (American writer)

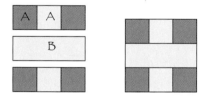

Diagram 1

Diagram 2

Diagram 3

Diagram 4

Sashing Row Assembly Diagram

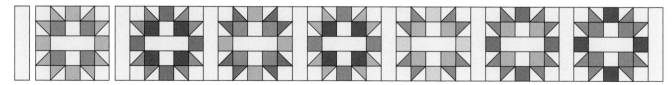

Block Row Assembly Diagram

Sister's Choice
BLOCK BY BLOCK

Instructions for 1 (10")
Sister's Choice Block

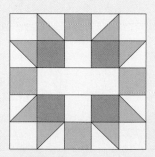

Block Diagram

MATERIALS
4 (2½") dark print squares (A)
2 (2½") muslin squares (A)
1 (2½" x 6½") muslin rectangle (B)
4 (2½") medium #2 print squares (A)
4 (2⅞") medium #1 print squares (C)
4 (2⅞") light print squares (C)
4 (2½") light print squares (A)

CUTTING
Cut 8 (2⅞") squares in half diagonally to make 16 half-square triangles C.

BLOCK ASSEMBLY
Refer to *Block Assembly Diagram* throughout.
1. Join 4 dark As, 2 muslin As, and 1 muslin B to make center section (*Diagram 1*).
2. Join 1 light C and 1 medium #1 C to make 1 half-square triangle unit (*Diagram 2*). Make 8 C half-square triangle units.
3. Join 1 C unit to each side of 1 medium #2 A square (*Diagram 3*). Make 4 A/C strips.
4. Join 1 light A square to each end of 1 A/C strip to make top strip (*Diagram 4*). Repeat for bottom strip.
5. Join 1 A/C strip to each side of center section as shown.
6. Join 1 top strip and 1 bottom strip to block as shown to complete. Block should measure 10½". Sign block.

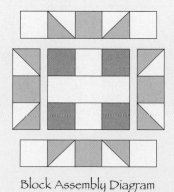

Block Assembly Diagram

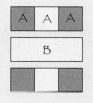

Diagram 1

Diagram 2

Diagram 3

Diagram 4

Hands of Friendship

A new job in Georgia moved Elizabeth Holloway from her home in Chapel Hill, North Carolina. As a going-away present, the ladies in Elizabeth's quilting bee made this quilt for her. Each person appliquéd her handprint and a heart on a piece of muslin, making a friendship block. Each heart has the maker's name or a short message. "They needed two extra blocks, so they traced my daughter's hands and mine," Elizabeth says. "On my block I wrote 'Gone to Carolina in My Mind,' which is the name of one of my favorite songs and the perfect explanation of my feelings."

Hands of Friendship

Finished Size: 36" x 54½"
Blocks: 12 (8" x 10") Hands of Friendship Blocks

Materials
1½ yards total assorted plaids for
   blocks and border
1 yard muslin for blocks
1 yard red print for sashing,
   border, and binding (1½ yards
   for unpieced borders)
1¾ yards cream print for
   backing
Crib-size batting

Cutting
Measurements include ¼" seam
allowances. Border strips are exact
length needed. You may want to
cut them longer to allow for piecing variations. Cut fabric selvage to
selvage unless otherwise noted.

From assorted plaids, cut:
• 12 (8" x 10") rectangles.
• 12 sets of 2 (1" x 10½") side
  borders and 2 (1" x 9½") top
  and bottom borders
• 44 assorted 2" x 4½" rectangles
  for outer border.

From muslin, cut:
• 3 (8½"-wide) strips. Cut strips
  into 12 (8½" x 10½") rectangles for block backgrounds.
• 12 hearts in assorted shapes
  and sizes.

From red print, cut:
• 9 (2"-wide) strips. Cut and
  piece as necessary to make 2
  (2" x 49") side borders, 2 (2" x
  33½") top and bottom borders,
  3 (2" x 30½") horizontal sashing strips, and 8 (2" x 11½")
  vertical sashing strips. If you
  prefer unpieced borders, cut 2

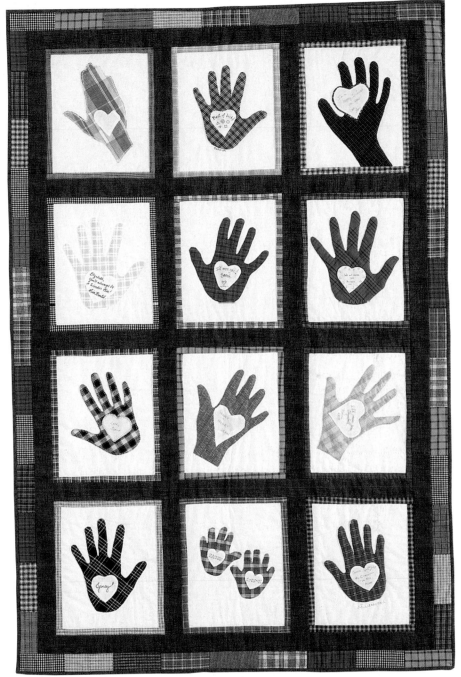

Janay Alford designed this quilt for Elizabeth Holloway. Other women who made
blocks and helped with the quilting are Sarah Williams, Gayle Rose, Marni
Goldshlag, Deborah Hauser, Sharon LeSoine, Amy Lanou, Nancy Smith, Jean
Miller, and Lisa Kroutil.

(2"-wide) lengthwise strips
from alternate yardage for side
borders. Proceed with crosswise
strips from remainder for
remaining strips and binding.
• 5 (2¼"-wide) strips for binding.

Block Assembly
1. Trace around hand on 1 plaid
rectangle. Cut out and appliqué to
1 (8½" x 10½") muslin rectangle.
2. Appliqué 1 heart with name and
sentiments as desired.

Hands of Friendship

3. Add 1 (1" x 10½") plaid border to each side. Add 1 (1" x 9½") plaid border to top and bottom. Plaid border should not match plaid hand.

4. Make 12 Hands of Friendship blocks.

Quilt Assembly

1. Alternate 3 blocks and 2 vertical sashing strips. Join into a row; make 4 block rows. Join rows with horizontal sashing strips to complete center.

2. Measure to ensure that borders will fit. Join 2 (2" x 49") red print borders to quilt sides. Add 2 (2" x 33½") red print borders to top and bottom of quilt.

3. Join plaid rectangles into 2 (9-unit) strips and 2 (13-unit) pieced plaid border strips as shown. Measure, trim, and add pieced plaid borders to quilt sides, and then to top and bottom.

Quilting and Finishing

1. Layer backing, batting, and quilt top; baste. Quilt as desired. Quilt shown was quilted in-the-ditch around hands and blocks only.

2. Join 2¼"-wide red print strips into 1 continuous piece for straight-grain French-fold binding. Add binding to quilt.

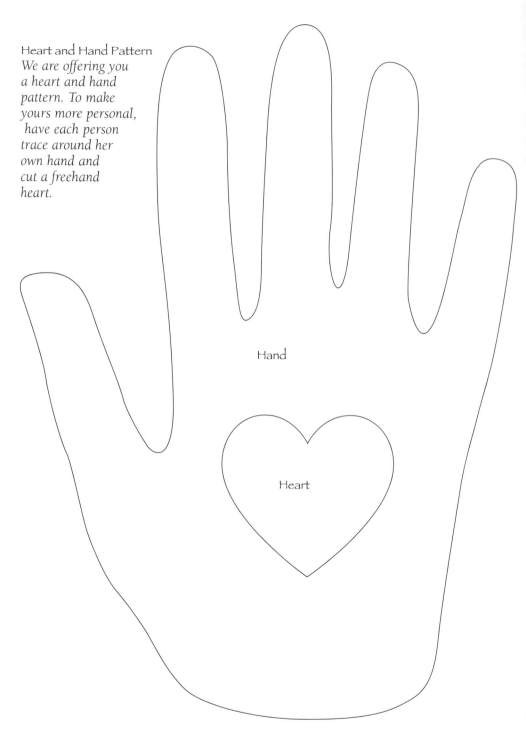

Heart and Hand Pattern
We are offering you a heart and hand pattern. To make yours more personal, have each person trace around her own hand and cut a freehand heart.

Hand

Heart

Hands of Friendship
BLOCK BY BLOCK

Instructions for 1 (8" x 10")
Hands of Friendship Block

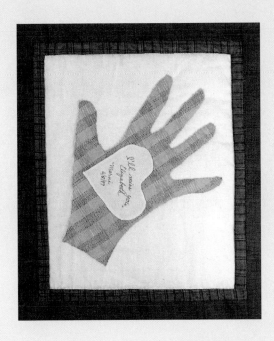

MATERIALS
1 (8" x 10") plaid rectangle
1 (8½" x 10½") muslin rectangle
1 muslin heart (cut freehand)
2 (1" x 10½") and 2 (1" x 9½")
  plaid strips

BLOCK ASSEMBLY
1. Trace around your hand on 1 plaid
rectangle. Cut out and appliqué to muslin
rectangle.
2. Sign and appliqué heart to hand.
3. Add 1 (1" x 10 ½") plaid border to each side.
Add 1 (1" x 9½") plaid border to top and bottom.
Plaid border should not match plaid hand. Block
should measure 8½" x 10½".

Make it your ambition

to lead a quiet life, to mind your own business

and to work with your hands.

—*I Thessalonians 4:11(NIV)*

Mary's Graduation Quilt

As graduation day for Marianne Fons's daughter approached, she started planning how to commemorate the event in fabric. "With major help from Liz Porter and my good friend Marty Freed, we cut, stitched, and readied blocks for signatures one day in mid-May," says Marianne. "At my daughter Mary's reception on graduation day, guests selected blocks from the design wall and wrote their good wishes. I finished the quilt in time for Mary to take it off to college to keep her warm. When I washed the quilt recently, I noticed she has added in one corner, 'One year later, and I still sleep well.'"

Mary's Graduation Quilt

Finished Size: 69¾" x 95¼"
Blocks: 59 (9") Puss in the Corner Blocks

Materials
30 fat quarters (18" x 22")
   assorted batik prints
5½ yards off-white fabric
¾ yard blue print for binding
6 yards fabric for backing
Full-size batting

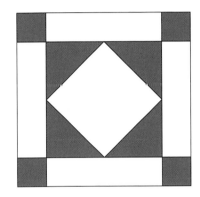

Block Diagram

Cutting
Measurements include ¼" seam allowances. Border strips are exact length needed. You may want to cut them longer to allow for piecing variations. Cut fabric selvage to selvage unless otherwise noted.

From assorted batik prints, cut:
- 59 sets (2 from each fabric) of:
  - 4 (3½") squares (A).
  - 4 (2") squares (D).
- From remainder, cut 22"-long strips ranging from 1½" to 4½"-wide for border.

From off-white, cut:
- 22 (6½"-wide) strips. Cut strips into 59 (6½") squares (B) and 236 (2" x 6½") rectangles (C).
- 2 (14"-wide) strips. Cut strips into 5 (14") squares. Cut squares in quarters diagonally to make 20 side setting triangles.
- 1 (7¼"-wide) strip. Cut strip into 2 (7¼") squares. Cut squares in half diagonally to make 4 corner setting triangles.

From blue print, cut:
- 9 (2¼"-wide) strips for binding.

This quilt offers a great opportunity to use those fat quarters of fabric that you've been collecting. You can piece the block quickly, if you have a deadline to meet.

Block Assembly
1. Using diagonal seams, join 1 A square to opposite corners of 1 B square (*Diagram 1*). Trim and open out (*Diagram 2*).
2. Join 1 A square to each remaining corner (*Diagram 3*). Trim and open out (*Diagram 4*).
3. Referring to *Block Assembly Diagram*, add 2 C strips to sides of

Mary's Graduation Quilt

block. Add 1 D square to each end of 2 C strips. Add to top and bottom of block to complete block.

4. Make 59 Puss in the Corner blocks (*Block Diagram*).

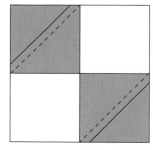

Diagram 1

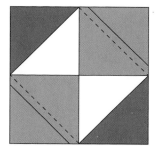

Diagram 3

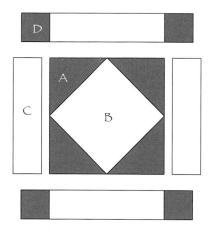

Block Assembly Diagram

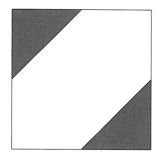

Diagram 2

Diagram 4

Quilt Assembly

1. Lay out blocks and setting triangles as shown in *Quilt Top Assembly Diagram*. Join into diagonal rows. Join rows to complete quilt.

2. Join random width 22"-long batik strips into strip sets about 12"-wide. Press seams to 1 side. From strip sets, cut $3\frac{1}{2}$"-wide segments. Join segments to form 2 ($3\frac{1}{2}$" x $89\frac{3}{4}$") side borders, 2 ($3\frac{1}{2}$" x $64\frac{1}{2}$") top and bottom borders, and 4 ($3\frac{1}{2}$") border corner squares.

3. Join $3\frac{1}{2}$" x $89\frac{3}{4}$" borders to quilt sides. Add border corners to ends of remaining borders. Join borders to quilt top and bottom.

Quilting and Finishing

1. Divide backing fabric into 2 (3-yard) lengths. Cut 1 piece in half lengthwise. Sew 1 narrow panel to each side of wide panel. Press seam allowances toward narrow panels.

2. Layer backing, batting, and quilt top; baste. Quilt as desired. Quilt shown was meander-quilted in sashing and setting triangles only.

3. Join $2\frac{1}{4}$"-wide blue print strips into 1 continuous piece for straight-grain French-fold binding. Add binding to quilt.

Quilt Top Assembly Diagram

Mary's Graduation Quilt

BLOCK BY BLOCK

Instructions for 1 (9")
Puss in the Corner Block

MATERIALS

8" x 12" scrap batik print
8" x 14" scrap off-white

CUTTING

From batik print, cut:

- 4 (3½") squares (A).
- 4 (2") squares (D).

From off-white, cut:

- 1 (6½") squares (B).
- 4 (2" x 6½") rectangles (C).

BLOCK ASSEMBLY

1. Using diagonal seams, join 1 A square to opposite corners of B square (*Diagram 1*). Trim and open out (*Diagram 2*).

2. Join 1 A square to each remaining corner (*Diagram 3*). Trim and open out (*Diagram 4*).

3. Referring to *Block Assembly Diagram,* add 2 C strips to sides of block. Add 1 D square to each end of 2 C strips. Add to top and bottom of block to complete block. Block should measure 9½". Sign block.

Block Diagram

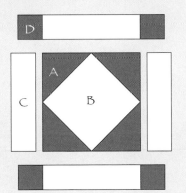

Block Assembly Diagram

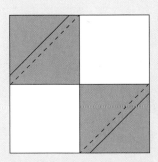

Diagram 1

Diagram 2

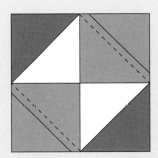

Diagram 3

Diagram 4

Irish Friendship Quilt

Mona Richards, of Birmingham, Alabama, made this quilt based on one she'd seen her grandmother make. "Our family has an Irish heritage, so the shamrocks naturally attracted me," says Mona. While her grandmother stitched the blocks directly to each other in rows, Mona chose to add kelly green sashing.

Irish Friendship Quilt

Finished Size: 65½" x 97"
Blocks: 54 (8") Shamrock Blocks

Materials
3 yards white for blocks
6 yards white for backing (or 2
    yards of 108"-wide backing)
4½ yards green for appliqué and
    sashing
Queen-size batting
Black and green embroidery
    thread

Block Diagram

Cutting
Measurements include ¼" seam
allowances. Sashing strips are exact
length needed. You may want to
cut them longer to allow for piecing variations. Cut fabric selvage to
selvage unless otherwise noted.

From white, cut:
• 11 (8½"-wide) strips. Cut strips
  into 54 (8½") background
  squares.

From green, cut:
• 2 yards. Cut 10 (3"-wide)
  lengthwise strips. Cut strips
  into 10 (3" x 66") horizontal
  sashing strips.
• 13 (3"-wide) strips. Cut strips
  into 63 (3" x 8½") sashing strips.
• 162 As.

*Legend says that St. Patrick used the shamrock in the fifth century to demonstrate
the meaning of the Trinity—that is, the Father, Son, and Holy Ghost are three
separate beings, and yet one, just as the shamrock is three leaves, yet one. The
word "shamrock" is derived from the Irish "seamrog," meaning "summer plant,"
and is Ireland's most famous symbol.*

Block Assembly
1. Using black embroidery floss,
blanket-stitch 3 shamrock leaves as
shown to 1 white background
block. Satin-stitch stem in green
(*Block Diagram*). Have block signed
and then embroider over signature
in green.

2. Make 54 Shamrock blocks.

Quilt Assembly
1. Alternate 7 sashing strips and 6
blocks as shown in *Row Assembly
Diagram*. Join into a row. Make 9 rows.

Row Assembly Diagram

2. Referring to photo, alternate block rows with horizontal sashing strips and join to complete quilt top.

Quilting and Finishing

1. Divide backing fabric into 3 (2-yard) lengths. Join along sides to make backing. Seams will run horizontally.

2. Layer backing, batting, and quilt top; baste. Quilt as desired. Quilt shown was quilted around leaves and stems and in-the-ditch around each block.

3. Trim batting even with quilt top. Trim backing to 2" around all sides of quilt.

4. Fold backing in half toward quilt and press. Fold again to front and slipstitch in place to make ½"-wide binding. Miter corners.

THE IRISH BLESSING

May the road rise to meet you,

May the wind be always at your back,

May the sun shine to warm your face,

The rains fall soft upon your fields,

And until we meet again,

May God hold you in the palm of His hand.

Irish Friendship Quilt
BLOCK BY BLOCK

Instructions for 1 (8")
Shamrock Block

MATERIALS
¼ yard white
⅛ yard or scrap green
Green and black embroidery floss

CUTTING
From white, cut:
- 1 (8½") square.

From green, cut:
- 3 As.

Block Diagram

BLOCK ASSEMBLY
Using black embroidery floss, blanket-stitch 3 shamrock leaves as shown to 1 white background block (*Block Diagram*). Satin stitch stem in green. Sign block. Embroider over signature in green.

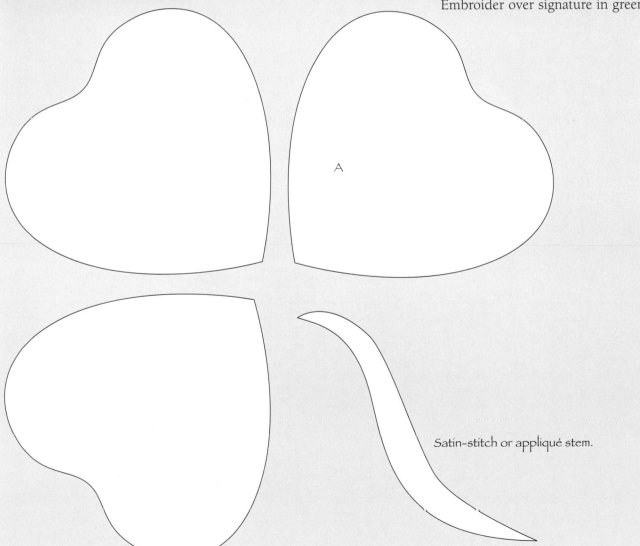

A

Satin-stitch or appliqué stem.

30th Birthday Bash

Milestone birthdays call for celebration. What better way to commemorate that celebration than with a quilt? When Rhonda Richards turned 30, she threw herself a party. Guests signed muslin triangles, which were later made into cake stand blocks. This colorful quilt, which hangs on her bedroom wall, is a cheerful reminder of friends and family. Machine-quilted by New Traditions.

30th Birthday Bash

Finished Size: 42" x 56½"
Blocks: 15 (8") Cake Stand Blocks

Materials

8 (6" x 14") assorted dark scraps
  for blocks
15 (3" x 9") and 8 (5" x 14")
  assorted light scraps for blocks
¼ yard muslin for blocks
1 yard gold print for setting
  triangles
1¾ yards blue stripe for sashing
  and binding
1¾ yards yellow-and-white plaid
  for backing
Crib-size batting

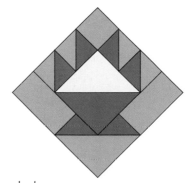

Block Diagram

Cake Stand blocks are ideal for commemorating a milestone birthday. Another option is to make as many blocks as the person has aged in years.

Cutting

Measurements include ¼" seam allowances. Cut fabric selvage to selvage unless otherwise noted.

From each dark scrap, cut:

- 1 (4⅞") square. Cut square in half diagonally to make 2 cake half-square triangles (C).
- 6 (2⅞") squares. Cut squares in half diagonally to make 12 B triangles.

From each 3" x 9" light scrap, cut:

- 2 (2⅞") squares. Cut squares in half diagonally to make 4 B triangles.
- 1 (2½") square (A).

From each 5" x 14" light scrap, cut:

- 1 (4⅞") square. Cut square in half diagonally to make 2 bottom C half-square triangles.
- 4 (2½" x 4½") D rectangles.

From muslin, cut:

- 8 (4⅞") squares. Cut squares in half diagonally to make 15 C triangles. You will have 1 extra.

From gold print, cut:

- 2 (12⅝"-wide) strips. Cut strips into 6 (12⅝") squares. Cut squares in quarters diagonally to make 24 side setting triangles.
- 1 (6⅝"-wide) strip. Cut strip into 6 (6⅝") squares. Cut squares in half diagonally to make 12 corner setting triangles.

30th Birthday Bash

From blue stripe, cut:
- 4 (2½"-wide) lengthwise strips for sashing. Center stripe for each strip.
- 4 (2¼"-wide) lengthwise strips for binding.

Block Assembly

1. For "cake" portion of each block, choose 1 A square and 4 B triangles in light prints, 4 B dark print triangles, 1 C dark print triangle, and 1 C muslin triangle.

2. Join pairs of light and dark B triangles to make 4 triangle-squares. Join C triangles in same manner.

3. Referring to *Block Assembly Diagram,* join B triangles in pairs as shown. Join 1 pair to top of C triangle-square as shown. Add A square to remaining pair and add to C as shown.

4. Join 2 B dark print triangles to ends of 2 D light print rectangles. Add to C unit as shown.

5. Add 1 C light print triangle to corner to complete block as shown in *Block Diagram.*

6. Make 15 Cake Stand blocks.

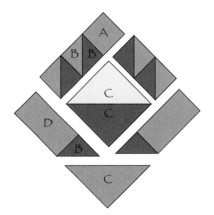

Block Assembly Diagram

Quilt Assembly

1. Lay out 5 blocks, 8 setting triangles, and 4 corner triangles as shown in first row of *Quilt Top Assembly Diagram.* Join into diagonal units; join units to make 1 vertical row. Make 3 vertical rows.

2. Alternate 4 sashing strips and 3 block strips as shown in *Quilt Top Assembly Diagram.* Join to complete quilt. Trim excess sashing.

Quilting and Finishing

1. Layer backing, batting, and quilt top; baste. Quilt as desired. Quilt shown was meander-quilted all over, avoiding muslin triangles.

2. Join 2¼"-wide blue strips into 1 continuous piece for straight-grain French-fold binding. Add binding to quilt.

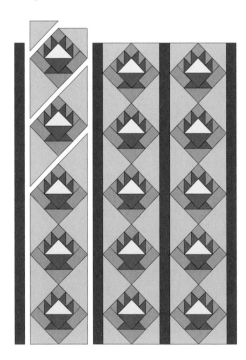

Quilt Top Assembly Diagram

PARTY PREPARATIONS!

Since the birthday party guests were not quilters, Rhonda Richards had to make preparations before the party. Here are her tips for making this quilt with friends:

- Cut twice as many muslin triangles (C) as needed, so guests won't be intimidated by the thought of "messing up" their block.

- Cut freezer-paper triangles ¼" smaller on all sides and press them to the back. Tell people to decorate their triangles only on the stabilized area, so that they won't accidentally write within the seam allowance.

- Set up an area with rubber stamps, fabric pens, and fabric-safe ink with the prepared triangles. As guests arrive, ask them to decorate triangles any way they want, but be sure to include their signatures.

- When ready to stitch the blocks, select fabrics in colors that suit each person. Rhonda knew she wanted the quilt to hang in her bedroom, so she set the blocks in yellow and blue to match the quilt on her bed.

"This is one of my favorite quilts," says Rhonda. "It is the first thing I see when I wake up in the morning, and it cheers me every time I look at it."

See Resources on page 160 for stamping and inking supplies, page 149 for stamping instructions, and page 150 for printing quilt labels on a computer.

30th Birthday Bash

BLOCK BY BLOCK

Instructions for 1 (8")
Cake Stand Block

MATERIALS

1 (6" x 11") dark scrap
1 (3" x 9") and 1 (5" x 14") assorted light scraps
1 (5") square muslin

CUTTING

From 6" x 11" dark print, cut:

- 1 (4⅞") square. Cut square in half diagonally to make 2 cake half-square triangles (C). You will have 1 extra.
- 3 (2⅞") squares. Cut squares in half diagonally to make 6 B triangles.

From 3" x 9" light scrap, cut:

- 2 (2⅞") squares. Cut squares in half diagonally to make 4 B triangles.
- 1 (2½") square (A).

From 5" x 14" light print, cut:

- 1 (4⅞") square. Cut square in half diagonally to make 2 bottom C half-square triangles. You will have 1 extra.
- 2 (2½" x 4½") D rectangles.

From muslin, cut:

- 1 (4⅞") square. Cut square in half diagonally to make 1 C triangle. You will have 1 extra.

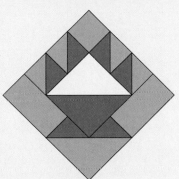

Block Diagram

BLOCK ASSEMBLY

1. For "cake" portion of each block, choose 1 A square and 4 B triangles in light prints, 4 B dark print triangles, 1 C dark print triangle, and 1 C muslin triangle.

2. Join pairs of light and dark B triangles to make 4 triangle-squares. Join C triangles in same manner.

3. Referring to *Block Assembly Diagram,* join B triangles in pairs as shown. Join 1 pair to top of C triangle-square as shown. Add A square to remaining pair and add to C as shown.

4. Join 2 B dark print triangles to ends of 2 D light print rectangles. Add to C unit as shown.

5. Add 1 C light print triangle to corner to complete block as shown in *Block Diagram*. Sign block.

Block Assembly Diagram

Album of Memories

"In 1946, it seemed that life was handing me scraps," says Alvina Nelson, of Salina, Kansas. "Life was not going well, and I was very unhappy. So I followed the saying, 'When life gives you scraps, make a quilt,' and this quilt is the result." Alvina collected signatures from relatives, friends, teachers, and coworkers over several years. "I would ask the person to sign in pencil, and then I embroidered over their names afterwards."

Album of Memories

Finished Size: 80" x 90"
Blocks: 56 (7") Friendship Blocks

Materials
3½ yards blue
6 yards white
5½ yards white for backing
Full-size batting
Blue embroidery floss

Cutting
Measurements include ¼" seam allowances. Border strips are exact length needed. You may want to cut them longer to allow for piecing variations. Cut fabric selvage to selvage unless otherwise noted.

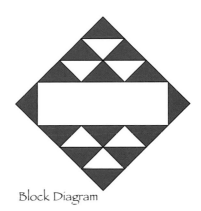

Block Diagram

From blue, cut:
- 25 (2⅝"-wide) strips. Cut strips into 392 (2⅝") squares. Cut squares in half diagonally to make 784 half-square triangles (A).
- 4 (5½"-wide) strips. Cut strips into 26 (5½") border squares.
- 2 (3"-wide) strips. Cut strips into 16 (3") corner border squares.
- 9 (2¼"-wide) strips for binding.

From white, cut:
- 11 (2⅝"-wide) strips. Cut strips into 168 (2⅜") squares. Cut squares in half diagonally to

Alvina Nelson arranged the blocks in alphabetical order. "One of the white setting blocks has a signature because a dear friend of mine, who was visiting while I was quilting, wondered why her name was not included," says Alvina. "Since she was also a quilter, I had her sign her name on a white setting block, and I embroidered over it before I quilted any more. The same is true for the setting block with my name. It has two dates—the year I started the quilt and the year it was finished."

make 336 half-square triangles (A).
- 4 (8"-wide) strips. Cut strips into 56 (3" x 8") rectangles (B).
- 9 (7½"-wide) strips. Cut strips into 42 (7½") setting blocks.
- 5 (5½"-wide) strips. Cut strips into 30 (5½") border squares.
- 2 (3"-wide) strips. Cut strips into 16 (3") corner border squares.
- 3 (11¼"-wide) strips. Cut strips into 7 (11¼") squares. Cut squares in quarters diagonally to make 28 side setting triangles.

You will have 2 extra.
- 2 (5⅞") squares. Cut squares in half diagonally to make 4 corner setting triangles.

Block Assembly
Refer to *Block Assembly Diagram* throughout.
1. Join 1 blue A triangle and 1 white A triangle into a square. Make 6 squares.
2. Join 3 squares and 3 blue A triangles into a corner unit as shown. Make 2 corner units.

Album of Memories

3. Join 1 blue A triangle to each end of 1 white B rectangle.

4. Join corner units to each side of B unit to complete Friendship block as shown in *Block Diagram*.

5. Make 56 Friendship blocks.

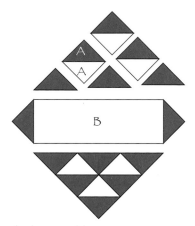

Block Assembly Diagram

Quilt Assembly

1. Lay out pieced blocks, setting blocks, and setting triangles as shown in *Quilt Top Assembly Diagram*. Join into diagonal rows; join rows.

2. Alternate 8 white and 7 blue 5½" squares; join to make 1 side border strip. Join 1 blue and 1 white 3" square; repeat. Add to ends of border strip as shown. Repeat for opposite side. Add to quilt sides.

3. Alternate 7 white and 6 blue 5½" squares; join to make 1 top border strip. Join 1 blue and 1 white 3" square; repeat to make 6 units. Join 3 units as shown and add to 1 end of top border strip. Repeat for opposite end. Join to top of quilt, matching seams.

4. Repeat Step 3 for bottom border.

Quilting and Finishing

1. Divide backing into 2 (2¾-yard) lengths. Cut 1 piece in half lengthwise. Sew 1 narrow panel to each side of wide panel. Press seam allowances toward narrow panels.

2. Layer backing, batting, and quilt top; baste. Quilt as desired. Quilt shown was outline-quilted in white areas of blocks. A fleur-de-lis pattern (see page 71) was used in setting blocks and triangles, and a wave pattern appears in border. Names are embroidered in blue.

3. Join 2¼"-wide blue strips into 1 continuous piece for straight-grain French-fold binding. Add binding to quilt.

> *It is easy to be independent when you've got money. But to be independent when you haven't got a thing— that's the Lord's test.*
>
> —Mahalia Jackson (American gospel singer)

Quilt Top Assembly Diagram

Tribute to My Mother

by Alvina Nelson

Stitching by hand for many an hour
As she sits by the south bay window
And listens to a soap opera
on the radio,
I can still picture my mother
Piecing together a beautiful quilt.

Silently needle and thread glide
Through colorful fabrics
of many designs,
Pieces cut into many
different shapes.

As she stitches away, cares
and stress disappear.
For that was her theory—
"It was good to play with thread."

I, too, find this to be true.
Today, when life hands me scraps,
I cut, stitch, and quilt for hours on
end 'til many a care disappears
As yet another quilt appears.

Today, she is no longer with us.
A Flower Garden quilt reminds
me of her.
For she loved her flowers and quilts
And shared them with us all.

I am blessed with her memory.
Her love of stitching
Lives on in my quilts.

Someday, when my life here
on earth is ended,
I'll hope to meet my mother again.
We'll chat of times long ago
and times more recent.
And, Mother, I hope you'll
be pleased
With my stitches that have traveled
many a mile

Album of Memories

BLOCK BY BLOCK

Instructions for 1 (7")
Friendship Block

MATERIALS
1 fat eighth (9" x 22") each
blue and white

CUTTING
From blue, cut:
- 7 (2⅝") squares. Cut squares in half diagonally to make 14 half-square triangles (A).

From white, cut:
- 3 (2⅝") squares. Cut squares in half diagonally to make 6 half-square triangles (A).
- 1 (3" x 8") rectangle (B).

BLOCK ASSEMBLY
1. Join 1 blue A triangle and 1 white A triangle into a square. Make 6 squares.
2. Join 3 squares and 3 blue A triangles into a corner unit as shown. Make 2 corner units.
3. Join 1 blue A triangle to each end of 1 white B rectangle.
4. Join corner units to each side of B unit to complete Friendship block (*Block Diagram*).
5. Block should measure 7½". Sign block.

Block Diagram

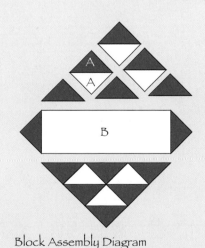

Block Assembly Diagram

Post Office Quilt

Postmaster Dyann Roby of Muscatine, Iowa, commissioned Kristin McHugh-Johnston to make this quilt to commemorate the opening of Muscatine's new post office. Dyann's only requirements for the quilt were that it needed to be red, white, and blue, with stars. Kristin developed a nine-patch friendship star quilt, and the 68 employees at the post office each signed a block. The quilt made its public debut at the post office's open house.

Post Office Quilt

Finished Size: 108" x 96"
Blocks: 72 (12") Milky Way Blocks

Materials
4 yards white-on-white for stars
4 yards red mottled print for
  background and binding
4 yards blue mottled print for
  background and binding
9¾ yards red, white, and blue
  print for backing
King-size batting

Blue Block
Diagram

Red Block
Diagram

The Americana color scheme used in this quilt makes it ideal for veterans' groups or patriotic holiday celebrations. The large block is easy to piece.

Cutting
Measurements include ¼" seam allowances. Cut fabric selvage to selvage unless otherwise noted.

From white-on-white, cut:
- 18 (4⅞"-wide) strips. Cut strips into 144 (4⅞") squares. Cut squares in half diagonally to make 288 half-square triangles.
- 8 (4½"-wide) strips. Cut strips into 72 (4½") squares.

From red mottled print, cut:
- 9 (4⅞"-wide) strips. Cut strips into 72 (4⅞") squares. Cut squares in half diagonally to make 144 half-square triangles.
- 16 (4½"-wide) strips. Cut strips into 144 (4½") squares.
- 5 (2¼"-wide) strips for binding.

From blue mottled print, cut:
- 9 (4⅞"-wide) strips. Cut strips into 72 (4⅞") squares. Cut

squares in half diagonally to make 144 half-square triangles.
- 16 (4½"-wide) strips. Cut strips into 144 (4½") squares.
- 5 (2¼"-wide) strips for binding.

Block Assembly
1. Join 1 blue half-square triangle to 1 white half-square triangle along long sides. Repeat to make 4 triangle-squares.
2. Arrange 4 triangle-squares, 1 white 4½" square, and 4 blue 4½" squares as shown in *Block Assembly Diagram*. Join into rows; join rows to complete 1 blue Milky Way block (*Block Diagram*).
3. Make 36 blue Milky Way blocks and 36 red Milky Way blocks.

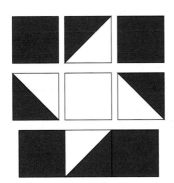

Block Assembly Diagram

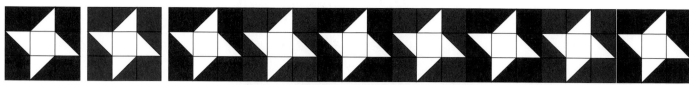

Row Assembly Diagram

Quilt Assembly

1. Alternate 5 red blocks and 4 blue blocks. Join into a row as shown in *Row Assembly Diagram*. Make 4 rows.
2. Alternate 5 blue blocks and 4 red blocks. Join into a row. Make 4 rows.
3. Alternate block rows as shown in photo and join to complete quilt top.

Quilting and Finishing

1. Divide backing fabric into 3 (3¼-yard) lengths. Join along sides to make backing. Seams will run horizontally.
2. Layer backing, batting, and quilt top; baste. Quilt as desired. Quilt shown was quilted in loops and stars in an allover pattern.
3. Join 2¼"-wide red and blue strips alternately into 1 continuous piece for straight-grain French-fold binding. Add binding to quilt.

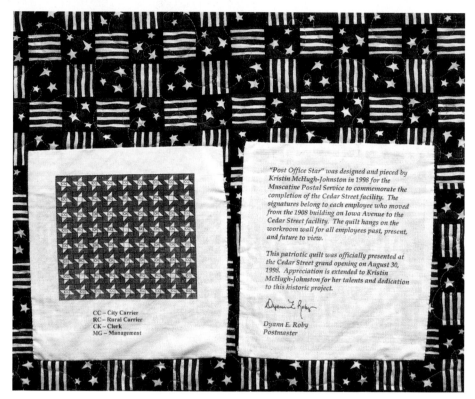

The quilt label for the Post Office Quilt includes a "map" of the quilt front, reflecting the positions of all the employees. A letter of dedication tells the story behind the quilt. See page 150 for information on making a computer-generated quilt label.

You don't know a woman until you have had a letter from her.

—Ada Leverson (English writer)

Post Office Quilt
BLOCK BY BLOCK

Instructions for 1 (12")
Milky Way Block

Blue Block Diagram

Red Block Diagram

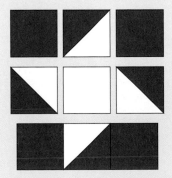

Block Assembly Diagram

MATERIALS

1 fat eighth (9" x 22") white-on-white
¼ yard red or blue mottled print

CUTTING

From white-on-white, cut:
- 2 (4⅞") squares. Cut squares in half diagonally to make 4 half-square triangles.
- 1 (4½") square.

From red or blue, cut:
- 2 (4⅞") squares. Cut squares in half diagonally to make 4 half-square triangles.
- 4 (4½") squares.

BLOCK ASSEMBLY

1. Join 1 red or blue half-square triangle to 1 white half-square triangle along long sides. Repeat to make 4 triangle-squares.

2. Arrange 4 triangle-squares, 1 white 4½" square, and 4 red or blue 4½" squares as shown. Join into rows; join rows to complete 1 Milky Way block. Block should measure 12½". Sign block.

Fond Memories

Helen Blakeley, of Scarborough, Ontario, began Fond Memories *as a signature quilt for students who attended St. Marys Collegiate Institute in St. Marys, Ontario, Canada. Helen took the top to their 1997 high school reunion for her former classmates to sign. After the 2000 reunion, Helen will donate the quilt to St. Marys Museum.*

Fond Memories

Finished Size: 61" x 67¾"
Blocks: 90 (5¼") Friendship Name Chain Blocks

Materials
2 yards total assorted red prints
4 yards white fabric
1¾ yards red check for border, binding, and hanging tabs
4 yards fabric for backing*
Twin-size batting

*Helen Blakeley chose to make the back of her quilt a photo transfer quilt. See page 144.)

Block Diagram

Helen Blakeley collected signatures of her fellow students at a class reunion in 1997. She incorporated the signatures into Friendship Name Chain blocks, shown here. Notice how the blocks create a lattice effect when joined. The reverse side of the quilt features photo transfer (see page 144).

Cutting
Measurements include ¼" seam allowances. Cut fabric selvage to selvage unless otherwise noted.

From assorted red prints, cut:
- 17 (2⅝"-wide) strips. Cut strips into 270 (2⅝") squares. Cut squares in half diagonally to make 540 half-square triangles (B) for blocks.
- 4 (2¾"-wide) strips. Cut strips into 61 (2¾") squares. Cut squares in half diagonally to make 122 half-square triangles for pieced border.

From white, cut:
- 1½ yards. Cut 4 (3¼"-wide) lengthwise strips. Cut strips into 4 (3¼" x 54") border strips.
- From remainder of 1½ yard, cut 9 (6"-wide) crosswise strips. Cut strips into 45 As.
- 7 (6"-wide) strips. Cut strips into 45 As. You will need 90 As in all.
- 6 (2⅝"-wide) strips. Cut strips into 90 (2⅝") squares. Cut squares in half diagonally to make 180 half-square triangles (B).
- 4 (2¾"-wide) strips. Cut strips into 61 (2¾") squares. Cut squares in half diagonally to

make 122 half-square triangles for pieced border.
- 4 (2⅜") pieced border corner squares.

From red check, cut:
- 2 (2¾"-wide) lengthwise strips for side borders.
- 2 (3½"-wide) lengthwise strips for top and bottom borders.
- 3 (4½"-wide) strips from remainder. Cut strips into 9 (4½" x 9½") rectangles for hanging tabs (optional).
- From remainder, cut (2¼"-wide) bias strips for binding.

Fond Memories

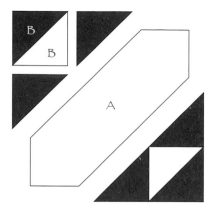

Block Assembly Diagram

Quilt Top Assembly Diagram

Block Assembly

Refer to *Block Assembly Diagram* throughout.

1. Join 1 red B to 1 white B to make 1 square.

2. Join 1 red B to 2 adjacent sides of square as shown to make 1 triangle unit.

3. Repeat to make 2 triangle units.

4. Join to each side of 1 A to complete block.

5. Make 90 Friendship Name Chain blocks (*Block Diagram*).

Quilt Assembly

1. Referring to *Quilt Top Assembly Diagram*, lay out blocks in 10 horizontal rows of 9 blocks each, turning blocks as shown. Join into rows; join rows to complete center.

2. Measure to ensure that borders will fit. Join 2 (3¼" x 53") white borders to sides of quilt. Add 2 (3¼" x 53¼") borders to top and bottom of quilt.

3. Join 1 red and 1 white border half-square triangle to make 1 square. Make 122 squares.

4. Join into 2 (29-unit) strips and 2 (32-unit) strips. Add 32-unit strips to sides of quilt. Add 1 corner square to each end of 29-unit strips. Add to top and bottom of quilt.

5. Measure quilt. Add 2¾"-wide red check borders. Trim as needed. Add 3½"-wide red check borders to top and bottom of quilt. Trim as needed.

Quilting and Finishing

1. Divide backing fabric into 2 (2-yard) lengths. Cut 1 piece in half lengthwise. Sew 1 narrow panel to 1 side of wide panel. Press seam allowances toward narrow panel. Remaining panel is extra.

2. Layer back, batting, and quilt top; baste. Quilt as desired. Quilt shown was quilted in-the-ditch in all triangles and outline-quilted in white signature area of each block. White border features a leaf and

vine pattern.

3. *For optional hanging tabs:* Fold 1 (4½" x 9½") rectangle in half lengthwise, with right sides facing. Stitch long side. Turn and press, centering seam on 1 side. Make 9 hanging tabs. Fold each tab in half to make a loop. Place tabs evenly across top edge of back with raw edges aligned. Stitch in place.

4. Join 2¼"-wide red check bias strips into 1 continuous piece for bias French-fold binding. Add binding to quilt, covering tab ends.

(See page 144 for quilt's reverse side that features photo transfer.)

Fond Memories

BLOCK BY BLOCK

Instructions for 1 (5¼")
Friendship Name Chain Block

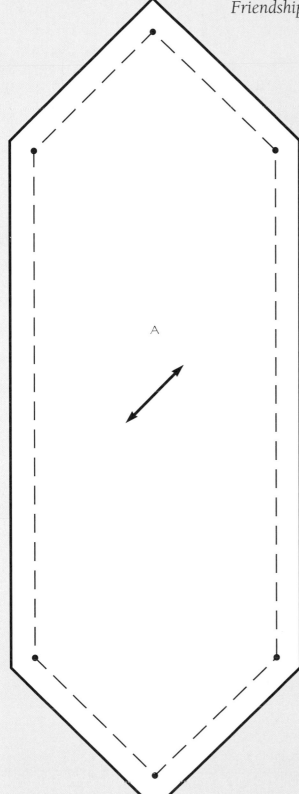

Helen added memorabilia to her quilt, such as old school pins and recognition pieces. She included information about each piece on the block to which it was attached.

MATERIALS

1 white A

1 (2⅝") white square. Cut square in half diagonally to make 2 white Bs.

3 (2⅝") red print squares. Cut squares in half diagonally to make 6 red Bs.

BLOCK ASSEMBLY

Refer to *Block Assembly Diagram* throughout.

1. Join 1 red B to 1 white B to make 1 square.

2. Join 1 red B to 2 sides of square as shown to make 1 triangle unit.

3. Repeat to make 2 triangle units.

4. Join to each side of 1 A to complete block. Block should measure 5¾" square. Sign block.

Block Diagram

Block Assembly Diagram

Friendship Star

Mona Richards found this antique quilt in a small shop in Harrison, Arkansas, while she was camping in the Ozarks. Research indicated that the pattern was first published in the 1930s under the name Friendship Star. Quiltmaker unknown; owned by Mona Richards.

Friendship Star

Finished Size: 66" x 77"
Blocks: 42 (11") Friendship Star
Blocks

Materials
3 yards total assorted 1930s
  prints for blocks (or 24 fat
  eighths*)
4 yards solid yellow for blocks
  and binding
4 yards fabric for backing
Twin-size batting
*Fat eighth = 9" x 22"

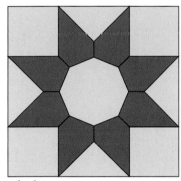

Block Diagram

Cutting
Measurements include ¼" seam
allowances. Cut fabric selvage to
selvage unless otherwise noted.

From assorted 1930s prints, cut:
• 42 sets of 8 Bs.

From solid yellow, cut:
• 42 As.
• 6 (5⅞"-wide) strips. Cut strips
  into 42 (5⅞") squares. Cut
  squares in quarters diagonally
  to make 168 C quarter-square
  triangles.
• 16 (3¾"-wide) strips. Cut strips
  into 168 (3¾") D squares.
• 7 (2¼"-wide) strips for binding

Although we don't know the full names of the people who made these blocks, we do know that they took a lot of pride in their work. In addition to embroidering their names, notice how some added small flowers in the center of the blocks.

Block Assembly
1. Join 8 Bs into a circle as shown.
Add 1 A to center.
2. Set in C triangles on opposite
sides of block. Set in D squares in
each corner of block (*Block
Assembly Diagram*).
3. Make 42 Friendship Star blocks
(*Block Diagram*).

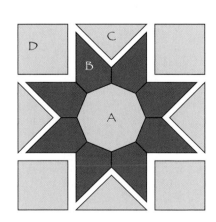

Block Assembly Diagram

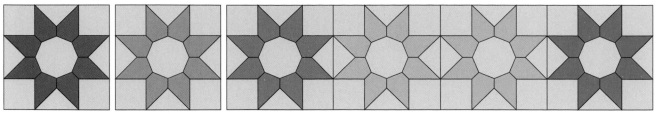

Row Assembly Diagram

Quilt Assembly

Using photo as a guide, arrange blocks in 7 horizontal rows of 6 blocks each. Join blocks into rows, as shown in *Row Assembly Diagram*. Join rows to complete quilt top.

Quilting and Finishing

1. Divide backing fabric into 2 (2-yard) lengths. Cut 1 piece in half lengthwise. Sew 1 narrow panel to each side of wide panel. Press seam allowances toward narrow panels. Seams will run horizontally.

2. Layer backing, batting, and quilt top; baste. Quilt as desired. Quilt shown was outline-quilted in centers, petals, and triangles. The yellow squares formed by 4 blocks coming together feature a star burst pattern.

3. Join 2¼"-wide yellow strips into 1 continuous piece for straight-grain French-fold binding. Add binding to quilt.

Make new friends,
but keep the old.
One is silver
and the other gold.

—*Source unknown*

A word fitly spoken is like apples of gold set in silver.

—*Proverbs 25:11*

Friendship Star
BLOCK BY BLOCK

Instructions for 1 (11")
Friendship Star Block

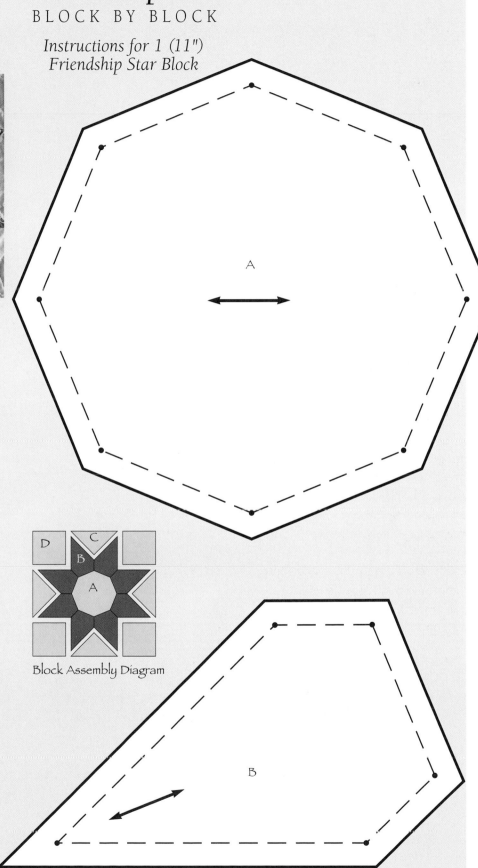

MATERIALS
1 fat eighth* or scrap 1930s
   print
1 fat eighth* solid yellow
*Fat eighth = 9" x 22"

CUTTING
From 1930s print, cut:
- 8 Bs.

From solid yellow, cut:
- 1 A.
- 4 (3¾") D squares.
- 1 (5⅞") square. Cut square in
  quarters diagonally to make 4
  C quarter-square triangles.

BLOCK ASSEMBLY
1. Join 8 Bs into a circle as
shown in *Block Assembly
Diagram*. Add 1 A to center.
2. Set in C triangles on opposite
sides of block. Set in D squares in
each corner of block to complete.
Block should measure 11½".
Sign block.

Block Assembly Diagram

Remember Me

Susan Cleveland began this quilt in a Mason-Dixon Memories workshop led by Marianne Fons. Since Susan used reproduction fabrics, she researched motifs and sayings such as "When this you see, remember me," popular during the Civil War, to embellish her blocks. Machine-pieced and hand-quilted by Susan Ramey Cleveland.

Remember Me

Finished Size: 56" x 69¼"
Blocks: 32 (8") Remember Me Blocks

Materials
32 fat eighths (9" x 22") assorted
  prints for blocks
½ yard muslin for blocks
1½ yards mottled tan for sashing
  and binding
¾ yard total assorted blue prints
  for sashing squares and setting
  triangles
½ yard total assorted pinks for
  setting triangles
4 yards mottled tan for backing
Twin-size batting

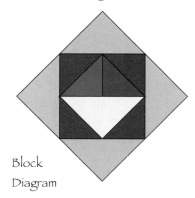

Block
Diagram

Cutting
Measurements include ¼" seam
allowances. Cut fabric selvage to
selvage unless otherwise noted.

From each assorted print, cut:
- 3 (3¾") squares. Cut squares in
  half diagonally to make 6 Bs.
- 2 (4⅞") squares. Cut squares in
  half diagonally to make 4 Cs.

From muslin, cut:
- 2 (7"-wide) strips. Cut strips
  into 8 (7") squares. Cut squares
  in quarters diagonally to make
  32 quarter-square triangles (A).

From mottled tan, cut:
- 16 (2"-wide) strips. Cut strips

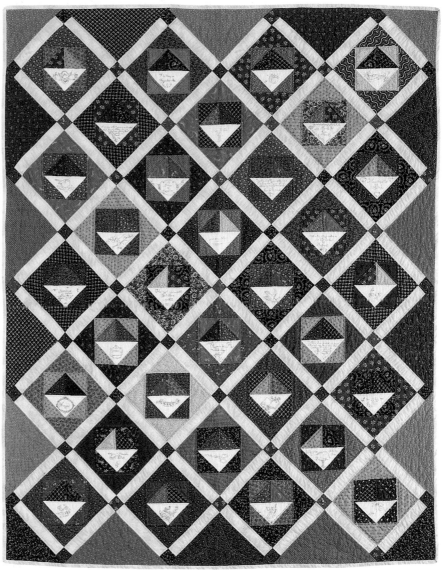

Because yardage of any one fabric was scarce, most Civil War quilts did not have borders. You can easily turn this lap quilt into a bed-sized quilt by adding borders to a modern version.

into 80 (2" x 8½") rectangles
for sashing.
- 7 (2¼"-wide) strips for binding.

From assorted blue prints, cut:
- 3 (2"-wide) strips. Cut strips
  into 49 (2") squares for sashing
  squares.
- 2 (14¾") squares. Cut squares
  in quarters diagonally to make
  8 side setting triangles. You will
  have 1 extra.

- 1 (8¾"-wide) square. Cut
  square in half diagonally to
  make 2 corner setting triangles.

From assorted pink prints, cut:
- 2 (14¾") squares. Cut squares
  in quarters diagonally to make
  8 side setting triangles. You will
  have 1 extra.
- 1 (8¾"-wide) square. Cut
  square in half diagonally to
  make 2 corner setting triangles.

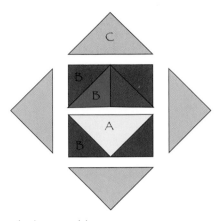

Block Assembly Diagram

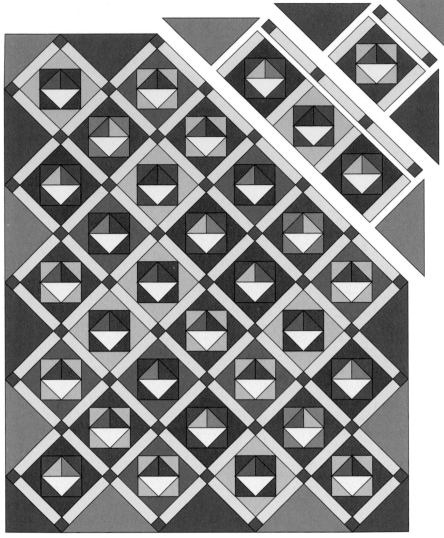

Quilt Top Assembly Diagram

Block Assembly

Refer to *Block Assembly Diagram* throughout.

1. Choose 1 A, 1 set of 4 matching Bs, 2 nonmatching Bs, and 1 set of 4 matching Cs. Join 2 matching Bs to each side of A. Join 1 matching B to 1 nonmatching B to make a square. Repeat with remaining Bs.

2. Join B squares and A unit as shown, with matching Bs to outside. Add 1 C to each side as shown to complete block.

3. Make 32 Remember Me blocks (*Block Diagram*).

Quilt Assembly

1. Lay out blocks, sashing strips, sashing squares, and setting triangles as shown in *Quilt Top Assembly Diagram*.

2. Join into diagonal rows. Join rows to complete quilt.

Quilting and Finishing

1. Divide backing fabric into 2 (2-yard) lengths. Cut 1 piece in half lengthwise. Sew 1 narrow panel to 1 side of wide panel. Remaining narrow panel is extra and can be used for a hanging sleeve.

2. Layer backing, batting, and quilt top; baste. Quilt as desired. Quilt shown was outline-quilted in blocks and sashing. Setting triangles have a feathered heart pattern.

3. Join 2¼"-wide mottled tan strips into 1 continuous piece for straight-grain French-fold binding. Add binding to quilt.

But godliness with contentment is great gain.

—1 Timothy 6:6 (NIV)

Remember Me
BLOCK BY BLOCK

Instructions for 1 (8")
Remember Me Block

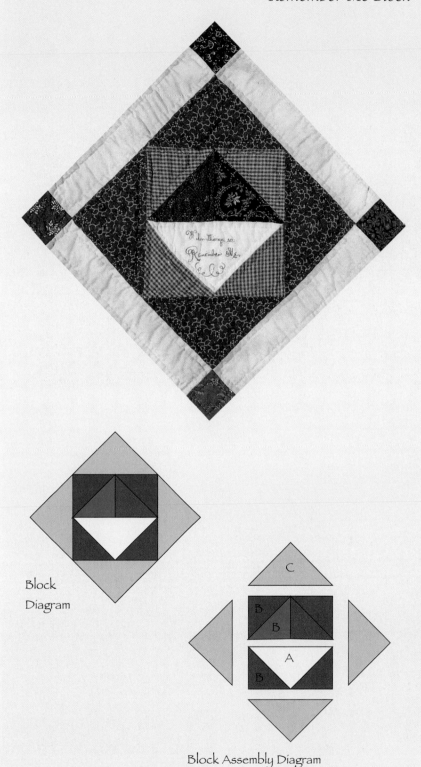

Block
Diagram

Block Assembly Diagram

MATERIALS
Fat eighths (9" x 22") or scraps of
  4 assorted prints
1 (7") square muslin

CUTTING
From each assorted print, cut:
- Fabric #1: 2 (3¾") squares. Cut
  squares in half diagonally to
  make 4 matching Bs.
- Fabric #2: 2 (4⅞") squares. Cut
  squares in half diagonally to
  make 4 matching Cs.
- Fabric #3: 1 (3¾") square. Cut
  square in half diagonally to
  make 2 Bs. You will have 1
  extra.
- Fabric #4: 1 (3¾") square. Cut
  square in half diagonally to
  make 2 Bs. You will have 1
  extra.

From muslin, cut:
- Square in quarters diagonally to
  make 4 quarter-square triangles
  (A). You will only need 1.

BLOCK ASSEMBLY
Refer to *Block Assembly Diagram*
throughout.
1. Join 2 matching Bs to each side
of A. Join 1 matching B to 1 nonmatching B to make a square.
Repeat with remaining Bs.
2. Join B squares and A unit as
shown, with matching Bs to outside. Add 1 C to each side as shown
to complete block. Block should
measure 8½". Sign block.

Antique Album Quilt

This quilt was presented to Rev. W. S. McAlilly, Gwen McAlilly Buckley's grandfather, in 1937. "The ladies of Whitehall Methodist Church in Louisville, Mississippi, made this quilt for him," says Gwen, "including blocks by my great aunts, cousins, and special family friends." He passed the quilt down to his son, Wendell McAlilly, who then passed it to his daughter Gwen.

Antique Album Quilt

Finished Size: 77¼" x 92¼"
Blocks: 30 (12¾") Album Blocks

Materials

40–60 fat quarters (18" x 22")
   assorted 1930s prints (half
   should be dark and half light)
2¾ yards solid green for sashing
   strips and borders
¼ yard solid pink for sashing
   squares
5½ yards white for backing
Full-size batting

Block Diagram

Cutting

Measurements include ¼" seam
allowances. Cut fabric selvage to
selvage unless otherwise noted.

**Choose 2 contrasting 1930s
prints for each block. From Fabric
#1 (background), cut:**

- 1 (2¾"-wide) strip. Cut strip
  into:
  - 2 (2¾") squares (A).
  - 1 (2¾" x 7¼") rectangle (B).
  - 2 (2½") squares. Cut squares
    in half diagonally to make 4 cor-
    ner triangles (D).
- 1 (4½"-wide) strip. Cut strip into
  3 (4½") squares. Cut squares in
  quarters diagonally to make 12
  quarter-square triangles (C) for
  block sides.

*This quilt prompted a family tradition in Gwen McAlilly Buckley's family. "We
have begun a system of family members making a block for a family quilt each
year," explains Gwen. "We draw to see who wins the blocks. The winner chooses
next year's design. We began with an Album quilt, of course!"*

From Fabric #2 (design), cut:

- 3 (2¾"-wide) strips. Cut strips
  into:
  - 8 (2¾") squares (A).
  - 4 (2¾" x 7¼") rectangles (B).
  Repeat to cut 30 sets of 2 fabrics.

From green, cut:

- 4 (2¾"-wide) lengthwise strips
  for outer borders.

- From remainder (31" width), cut
  25 (2¾"-wide) strips. Cut strips
  into 49 (2¾" x 13¼") rectangles
  for sashing strips.

From pink, cut:

- 2 (2¾"-wide) strips. Cut strips
  into 20 (2¾") sashing squares.

Antique Album Quilt

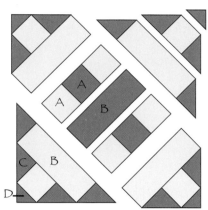

Block Assembly Diagram

Block Assembly

Refer to *Block Assembly Diagram* throughout.

1. Choose 1 set of Fabric #1 (background) and Fabric #2 (design) pieces. Join 2 design As to each side of 1 background A to make a strip. Repeat. Join 1 strip to each side of 1 background B to make center section.

2. Join 2 background C triangles to each side of 1 design A. Join to 1 design B. Add 1 background D triangle to complete side section. Repeat. Join side sections to center section.

3. Join 2 background C triangles to each side of 1 design A. Join 2 background C triangles to each side of 1 design B. Join as shown. Add 1 background D triangle to complete top section. Repeat for bottom section. Join to center section, matching seams.

4. Make 30 Album blocks in varying color combinations.

Quilt Assembly

1. Join 5 blocks and 4 green sashing strips as shown in *Row Assembly Diagram*. Make 6 rows.

2. Join 5 green sashing strips and 4 pink sashing squares as shown in *Sashing Assembly Diagram*. Make 5 sashing rows.

3. Referring to photo, alternate block rows and sashing rows; join to complete center.

4. Add 1 green border strip to each side of quilt, mitering corners.

Quilting and Finishing

1. Divide backing fabric into 2 (2¾-yard) lengths. Cut 1 piece in half lengthwise. Sew 1 narrow panel to each side of wide panel. Press seam allowances toward narrow panels.

2. Layer backing, batting, and quilt top; baste. Quilt as desired. Quilt shown was outline-quilted throughout.

3. Trim batting even with quilt top. Trim backing to 2" around all sides of quilt.

4. Fold backing in half toward quilt and press. Fold again to front and slipstitch in place to make ½"-wide binding. Miter corners.

Have not I commanded thee? Be strong and of good courage. Be not afraid, neither be thou dismayed, for the Lord thy God is with thee whithersoever thou goest.

—Joshua 1:9 (KJV)

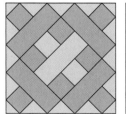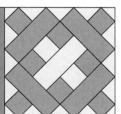

Row Assembly Diagram

Sashing Assembly Diagram

Antique Album Quilt

BLOCK BY BLOCK

Instructions for 1 (12¾")
Album Block

Block Diagram

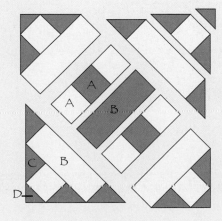

Block
Assembly
Diagram

MATERIALS
2 fat eighths (9" x 22") of coordinating
    1930s prints

CUTTING
From Fabric #1 (background), cut:
- 1 (2¾"-wide) strip. Cut strip into:
    - 2 (2¾") squares (A).
    - 1 (2¾" x 7¼") rectangle (B).
    - 2 (2½") squares. Cut squares in half diagonally to make 4 corner triangles (D).
- 1 (4½"-wide) strip. Cut strip into 3 (4½") squares. Cut squares in quarters diagonally to make 12 quarter-square triangles (C) for block sides.

From Fabric #2 (design), cut:
- 3 (2¾"-wide) strips. Cut strips into:
    - 8 (2¾") squares (A).
    - 4 (2¾" x 7¼") rectangles (B).

BLOCK ASSEMBLY
Refer to *Block Assembly Diagram* throughout.
1. Join 2 design As to each side of 1 background A to make a strip. Repeat. Join 1 strip to each side of 1 background B to make center section.
2. Join 2 background C triangles to each side of 1 design A. Join to 1 design B. Add 1 background D triangle to complete side section. Repeat. Join side sections to center section.
3. Join 2 background C triangles to each side of 1 design A. Join 2 background C triangles to each side of 1 design B. Join as shown. Add 1 background D triangle to complete top section. Repeat for bottom section. Join to center section, matching seams.
4. Block should measure 13¼". Sign block

Album Quilt

Linda Winter of Holdrege, Nebraska, combined traditional Album blocks to make her president's quilt. "Each quilt guild member gave me a piece of her favorite fabric, and I used it to make her block," says Linda. She collected signatures of guild members and special instructors who visited their guild.

Album Quilt

Finished Size: 85¾" x 85¾"
(excluding prairie points)
Blocks: 61 (8½") Album Blocks

Materials
32 fat eighths (9" x 22") assorted
   prints for blocks and prairie
   points
2¾ yards navy print for sashing
   and border
3½ yards white for blocks
7½ yards white for backing
Queen-size batting

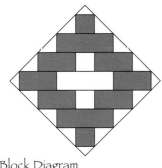

Block Diagram

Cutting
Measurements include ¼" seam
allowances. Cut fabric selvage to
selvage unless otherwise noted.

From assorted prints, cut:
- 2 sets of the following from
  each print for blocks:
  - 2 (2"-wide) strips. Cut strips
    into 2 (2") A squares, 2 (2" x
    5") B rectangles, and 6 (2" x
    3½") C rectangles.
- From remainder, cut 136 (3")
  squares for prairie points

From navy print, cut:
- 4 (2"-wide) lengthwise strips
  for borders.
- From remainder, cut 48 (2"-
  wide) selvage to selvage strips.
  Cut strips into 78 (2" x 9") F
  rectangles and 66 (2" x 10½")
  G rectangles.

In addition to making the signature blocks, Linda wrote special sayings in the setting and corner triangles, such as, "When this you see, remember me."

From white, cut:
- 14 (2"-wide) strips. Cut strips
  into 122 (2") A squares and 61
  (2" x 5") B rectangles.
- 13 (2¾"-wide) strips. Cut strips
  into 183 (2¾") squares. Cut
  squares in quarters diagonally
  to make 732 D quarter-square
  triangles. Handle gently; 2 sides
  are on the bias.
- 7 (2⅜"-wide) strips. Cut strips
  into 122 (2⅜") squares. Cut
  squares in half diagonally to
  make 244 E half-square triangles.
- 2 (14"-wide) strips. Cut strips
  into 5 (14") squares. Cut
  squares in quarters diagonally

to make 20 side setting
triangles (H).
- From remainder, cut 2 (7½")
  squares. Cut squares in half
  diagonally to make 4 corner
  setting triangles (I).

Block Assembly
Refer to *Block Assembly Diagram*
throughout.
1. Join 1 print C to each end of 1
white B. Join 1 white E to each end
of strip.
2. Join 1 print C to each end of 1
white A. Join 1 white D to each
end of strip as shown. Make 2
strips. Join 1 strip to each side of
B/C strip as shown.

Album Quilt

3. Join 1 white D to each end of 1 print B. Join 1 white D to opposite sides of 1 print A. Join A unit to B unit. Add 1 white E to top to complete A/B section. Make 2 A/B sections.

4. Join 1 A/B section to top and bottom of center section.

5. Join 1 navy F strip to top right edge of block. Add 1 G strip to top left edge of block to complete (*Block Diagram*).

6. Make 61 blocks.

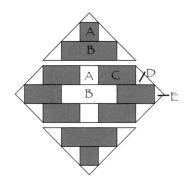

Block Assembly Diagram

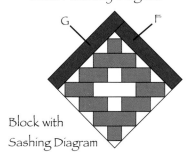

Block with Sashing Diagram

Setting Triangle Assembly

1. Referring to *Border Unit Diagrams,* join 1 F strip to top right edge of 1 H side setting triangle. Add 1 G strip to top left edge of 1 H side setting triangle. Make 5 bottom side setting triangle units.

2. Join 1 F strip to top edge of 1 H side setting triangle as shown. Make 5 left and 5 right side setting triangle units.

3. Join 1 F strip to 1 I corner setting triangle as shown. Make 2 bottom corner setting triangle units.

Quilt Assembly

1. Lay out blocks, side setting units and corner setting triangles as shown in photo. Join into diagonal rows; join rows to complete center. Setting triangles are oversized and will need to be trimmed.

2. Measure length of quilt from top E point to bottom E point (approximately 82¾"). Add ½" to measurement. Trim navy side borders to size, align with side E points, and add to opposite sides of quilt top. Trim excess from behind border. Measure width of quilt including border (approximately 86¼"). Trim two remaining navy borders to size. Join to top and bottom of quilt, aligning with top and bottom E points. Trim excess from behind border. Press seam allowance toward borders.

Quilting and Finishing

1. Divide backing fabric into 3 (2½-yard) lengths. Cut 1 piece in half lengthwise. Sew 1 narrow panel between wide panels. Press seam allowances toward narrow panel. Remaining panel is extra and may be used for a hanging sleeve.

2. Layer backing, batting, and quilt top; baste. Quilt as desired. Quilt shown was outline-quilted in prints and quilted in-the-ditch around blocks and in white areas. Setting triangles feature a chevron design.

3. Referring to *Prairie Point Diagrams,* fold 3" squares in half (*Diagram A*). Fold each piece in half again to make a small triangle (*Diagram B*).

4. On right side of quilt, arrange 34 prairie points along each side, one inside the next (*Diagram C*), aligned with border edge. Aligning raw edges of triangles and quilt

border, space prairie points evenly and baste through top and batting only, keeping backing free.

5. Folding backing out of the way, stitch prairie points in place through top and batting (*Diagram D*).

6. Trim batting even with quilt top. Trim backing 1" larger on all sides. Turn under raw edge of backing, covering raw edges of prairie points, and blindstitch backing in place (*Diagram E*).

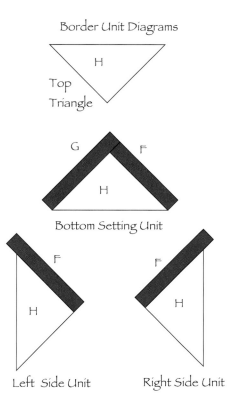

Border Unit Diagrams

Top Triangle

Bottom Setting Unit

Left Side Unit   Right Side Unit

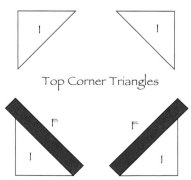

Top Corner Triangles

Bottom Corner Units

Prairie Point Diagrams

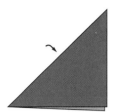

Diagram A

Diagram B

Diagram C

Diagram D

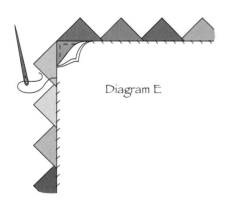

Diagram E

Album Quilt
BLOCK BY BLOCK

Instructions for 1 (8½")
Album Block

MATERIALS
1 fat sixteenth (4½" x 22")
  print
1 fat sixteenth (4½" x 22")
  white

CUTTING
From print, cut:
• 2 (2"-wide) strips. Cut strips into 2 (2") A squares, 2 (2" x 5") B rectangles, and 6 (2" x 3½") C rectangles.

Block Diagram

From white, cut:
• 3 (2¾") squares. Cut squares in quarters diagonally to make 12 D quarter-square triangles.
• 2 (2⅜") squares. Cut squares in half diagonally to make 4 E half-square triangles.
• 2 (2") A squares and 1 (2" x 5") B rectangle.

BLOCK ASSEMBLY
Refer to *Block Assembly Diagram* throughout.

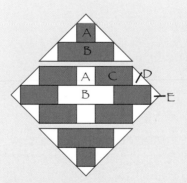

Block Assembly Diagram

1. Join 1 print C to each end of 1 white B. Join 1 white E to each end of strip.
2. Join 1 print C to each end of 1 white A. Join 1 white D to each end of strip as shown. Make 2 strips. Join 1 strip to each side of B/C strip as shown to complete center section.
3. Join 1 white D to each end of 1 print B. Join 1 white D to opposite sides of 1 print A. Join A unit to B unit. Add 1 white E to top to complete A/B section. Make 2 A/B sections.
4. Join 1 A/B section to top and bottom of center section.
5. Block should measure 9". Sign block.

Words of Wisdom for Ben

Faye Jahnel Bodenhamer, of Lino Lakes, Minnesota, made this quilt for her son's high school graduation. "In place of a guest book at Ben's graduation party, everyone was asked to sign a block and was encouraged to write something," she says. Along the inner muslin border, Faye wrote the names of his teachers and some famous quotes about wisdom. His Scout Master listed Ben's ranks. The four center blocks include his kindergarten and senior photo, his graduation invitation, and the "Class of 1997."

Words of Wisdom for Ben

Finished Size: 72" x 80"
Blocks: 72 (8") Star Blocks

Materials
48 fat eighths (9" x 22") assorted
 plaids for blocks
1¼ yards muslin
¾ yard brown plaid for border
 (2⅛ yards for unpieced
 borders)
¾ yard blue plaid for binding
5 yards small brown plaid
 backing
2 photos transferred to fabric
Twin-size batting

Block Diagram

Cutting
Measurements include ¼" seam allowances. Border strips are exact length needed. You may want to cut them longer to allow for piecing variations. Cut fabric selvage to selvage unless otherwise noted.

Choose 2 contrasting plaids for each block. From Fabric #1 (star), cut:

• 2 (1¾" x 4½") rectangles (B).
• 4 (2⅞") squares. Cut squares in half diagonally to make 8 half-square triangles (C).

From Fabric #2 (background), cut:

• 4 (2½") squares (D).
• 4 (2⅞") squares. Cut squares in

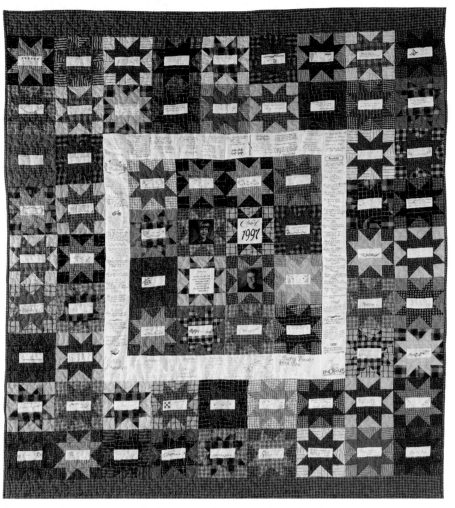

If you need to make a quilt for a man but have difficulty choosing an appropriate pattern, remember that fabrics can make a difference. The rustic plaids used in this quilt are ideal for a young man going to college.

half diagonally to make 8 half-square triangles (C).

• Cut 72 sets. In 4 sets of Fabric #1, omit B rectangles and substitute either 1 (4½") square muslin or 1 (4½") square photo transfer.

From muslin, cut:

• 4 (4½"-wide) strips. Cut strips into 2 (4½") squares for center blocks, 4 (4½") squares for center border, and 16 (4½" x 8½") rectangles for center border.
• 8 (2"-wide) strips. Cut strips

into 68 (2" x 4½") rectangles (A) for block strips.
• 2 (7") squares for photo transfer.

From brown plaid, cut:

• 4 (4½"-wide) strips. Piece to make 2 (4½" x 72½") top and bottom borders. If you prefer unpieced borders, cut 2 (4½"-wide) lengthwise strips from alternate yardage and trim to size.

From blue plaid, cut:

• 8 (2¼"-wide) strips for binding.

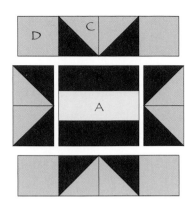

Block Assembly Diagram

Quilt Top Assembly Diagram

Block Assembly

Refer to *Block Assembly Diagram*.

1. Join 1 B to each side of 1 A to make center of block.

2. Join 2 contrasting C triangles into 1 triangle-square. Make 8 C triangle-squares.

3. Join C triangle-squares into pairs as shown. Join 1 pair to each side of A/B center. Join 1 D square to each end of remaining pairs. Add to top and bottom of block.

4. Make 68 Star blocks.

5. For remaining 4 blocks, omit center A/B unit, substituting 1 (4½") muslin square in 2 blocks and 1 (4½") square photo transfer in 2 blocks. See page 135 for photo transfer instructions and page 149 for lettering instructions.

Quilt Assembly

1. Lay out center section with 4 solid-center blocks and 12 Star blocks (*Quilt Top Assembly Diagram*). Join into rows as shown. Join rows to complete center.

2. Join 4 muslin rectangles into 1 center border strip. Repeat to make 4 center border strips. Add 1 strip to each side of center. Add 4 muslin squares to ends of remaining border strips; add to top and bottom of center.

3. Lay out remaining blocks in sections as shown. Join into rows; join rows to complete each section. Join side sections to center. Join top and bottom sections to quilt.

4. Add brown plaid border to top and bottom of quilt.

Quilting and Finishing

1. Divide backing fabric into 2 (2½-yard) lengths. Cut 1 piece in half lengthwise. Sew 1 narrow panel to each side of wide panel. Press toward narrow panels.

2. Layer backing, batting, and quilt top; baste. Quilt as desired. Quilt shown was quilted in an allover meander pattern, avoiding muslin.

3. Join 2¼"-wide blue plaid strips into 1 continuous piece for straight-grain French-fold binding. Add binding to quilt.

If any of you lacks wisdom, he should ask God, who gives generously to all without finding fault, and it will be given to him.

—*James 1:5 (NIV)*

Words of Wisdom
BLOCK BY BLOCK

Instructions for 1 (8")
Star Block

Block Diagram

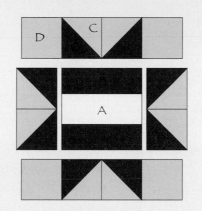

Block Assembly Diagram

MATERIALS

2 (6" x 12") rectangles assorted plaids
1 (2" x 4½") muslin rectangle (A)

CUTTING

From Fabric #1 (star), cut:
• 2 (1¾" x 4½") rectangles (B).
• 4 (2⅞") squares. Cut squares in half diagonally to make 8 half-square triangles (C).

From Fabric #2 (background), cut:
• 4 (2½") squares (D).
• 4 (2⅞") squares. Cut squares in half diagonally to make 8 half-square triangles (C).

BLOCK ASSEMBLY

1. Join 1 B to each side of 1 A to make center of block.
2. Join 2 contrasting C triangles into 1 triangle-square. Make 8 C triangle-squares.
3. Join C triangle-squares into pairs as shown. Join 1 pair to each side of A/B center. Join 1 D square to each end of remaining pairs. Add to top and bottom of block.
4. Block should measure 8½". Sign block.

Cardinals in Friendship Pines

Rolinda Collinson, of Friendship, Maryland, began this quilt by participating in a block-by-mail exchange group. She received 15 blocks from her sewing pen pals and then asked friends and relatives to also make blocks. "I supplied the muslin and the red 'cardinal' square," says Rolinda. "One person did not return the block, hence the 'goldfinch' in that tree!"

Cardinals in Friendship Pines

Finished Size: 74½" x 86"
Blocks: 30 (8") Pine Tree Blocks

Materials
3 yards total assorted greens and
    golds for blocks
⅛ yard total scraps assorted reds
    for blocks
¼ yard total scraps assorted
    browns for blocks
1¾ yards muslin for blocks
½ yard gold for border (2½ yards
    for unpieced borders)
¾ yard light green for border
    (2½ yards for unpieced
    borders)
2½ yards dark green for border
    and binding
5 yards muslin for backing
Full-size batting

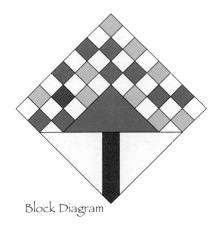

Block Diagram

When invited to participate in the block-by-mail group, Rolinda Collinson knew exactly what block she wanted everyone to make for her. She had always loved the Pine Tree block but never made it because of all the tiny 1"-squares involved. "We drew numbers and every four weeks the next person in line would send out the pattern for the block she wanted," says Rolinda. "I was ninth and received my first block in February 1994."

Cutting
Measurements include ¼" seam allowances. Border strips are exact length needed. You may want to cut them longer to allow for piecing variations. Cut fabric selvage to selvage unless otherwise noted.

From assorted greens and golds, cut:
• 540 (1½") squares.

From assorted reds, cut:
• 30 (1½") squares.

From assorted browns, cut:
• 30 (1½" x 5") rectangles (C).

From muslin, cut:
• 3 (6⅝"-wide) strips. Cut strips into 15 (6⅝") squares. Cut squares in quarters diagonally to make 60 B triangles for blocks.
• 22 (1½"-wide) strips. Cut strips into 600 (1½") squares for blocks.

From assorted greens, cut:
• 15 (4⅞") squares. Cut squares in half diagonally to make 30 block triangles (A).
• 20 (8½") squares for setting blocks.
• 5 (12⅝") squares. Cut squares in quarters diagonally to make 20 setting triangles. You will have 2 extra.
• 2 (6⅝") squares. Cut squares in half diagonally to make 4 corner setting triangles.

Cardinals in Friendship Pines

From gold, cut:
- 8 (1½"-wide) strips. Piece to make 4 (1½" x 86") border strips. If you prefer unpieced borders, cut 4 (1½"-wide) lengthwise strips from alternate yardage and trim to size.

From light green, cut:
- 8 (2½"-wide) strips. Piece to make 4 (2½" x 86") border strips. If you prefer unpieced borders, cut 4 (2½"-wide) lengthwise strips from alternate yardage and trim to size.

From dark green, cut:
- 4 (6½"-wide) lengthwise strips for outer border.
- 4 (2¼"-wide) lengthwise strips for binding.

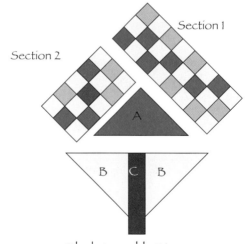

Block Assembly Diagram

Block Assembly

Refer to *Block Assembly Diagram* throughout.

1. Choose 18 assorted green and gold (1½") squares and 1 red 1½" square. Alternate colors with 20 muslin 1½" squares as shown. Join into rows; join rows to make Section 1 and Section 2. Join 1 green A triangle to Section 2 as shown. Join to Section 1.

2. Join 1 B triangle to each side of 1 C trunk. Add to block. Trim excess from small muslin squares on ends. Trim block to 8½" square.

3. Make 30 Pine Tree blocks.

Quilt Assembly

1. Lay out Pine Tree blocks, setting blocks, and setting triangles as shown in *Quilt Top Assembly Diagram.* Join into diagonal rows; join rows to complete center.

2. Join 1 gold border, 1 light green border, and 1 dark green border along long sides to make 1 border strip set. Make 4 sets.

3. Center each set on each side of quilt. Join to quilt, mitering corners.

Quilting and Finishing

1. Divide backing fabric into 2 (2½-yard) lengths. Cut 1 piece in half lengthwise. Sew 1 narrow panel to each side of wide panel. Press seam allowances toward narrow panels.

2. Layer backing, batting, and quilt top; baste. Quilt as desired. Quilt shown was grid-quilted in blocks, and in-the-ditch in borders. Outer border features purchased quilting stencils.

3. Join 2¼"-wide dark green strips into 1 continuous piece for straight-grain French-fold binding. Add binding to quilt.

Quilt Top Assembly Diagram

Cardinals in Friendship Pines
BLOCK BY BLOCK

Instructions for 1 (8")
Pine Tree Block

MATERIALS
18 (1½") assorted green and
  gold squares
1 (1½") red square
1 (1½" x 5") brown rectangle
1 fat eighth (9" x 22") muslin
1 (5") green square

CUTTING
From muslin, cut:
- 1 (6⅝") muslin square. Cut in
  quarters diagonally to make 4
  B triangles. You will have 2
  extra.
- 20 (1½") muslin squares.

From green, cut:
- 1 (4⅞") square. Cut in half
  diagonally to make 2 A triangles. You will have 1 extra.

BLOCK ASSEMBLY
1. Alternate green, gold, and red
squares with 20 muslin 1½"
squares as shown in *Block
Assembly Diagram*. Join into rows;
join rows to make Section 1 and
Section 2.
2. Join 1 green A triangle to
Section 2 as shown. Join to
Section 1.
3. Join 1 B triangle to each side of
1 C trunk. Add to block. Trim
excess from small muslin squares
on ends. Trim block to 8½"
square. Sign block.

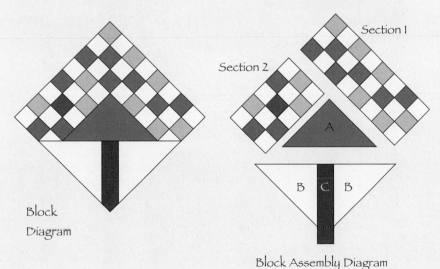

Block
Diagram

Section 1

Section 2

Block Assembly Diagram

Daisy Fan

Joyce Brown, of Philpot, Kentucky, wanted a fabric record of her family tree. She designed the blocks from two patterns her mother had used in quilts decades earlier. "I thought by using these patterns to design my own family genealogy quilt, it could be in honor of my mother and her quilting bee friends," Joyce says. She took the blocks to her family reunion and asked loved ones to sign them. Once all of the blocks were signed, Joyce pieced and hand-quilted the quilt.

Daisy Fan

Finished Size: 90" x 98"
Blocks: 90 (8") Daisy Fan Blocks

Materials

45 fat eighths (9" x 22") assorted prints for fans
4½ yards white for blocks
1 yard pink for inner border (2½ yards for unpieced borders)
2¾ yards red print for outer border
8¼ yards white fabric for backing
Queen-size batting
Embroidery floss to match prints

Block Diagram

When joined together, these blocks give the illusion of flowers—hence the name Daisy Fan.

Cutting

Measurements include ¼" seam allowances. Cut fabric selvage to selvage unless otherwise noted.

From assorted prints, cut:

• 90 sets of 4 As (2 sets from each print).

From white, cut:

• 18 (8½"-wide) strips. Cut strips into 90 (8½") squares for block backgrounds.

From pink, cut:

• 8 (3½"-wide) strips for inner border. Piece to make:

• 2 (3½" x 80½") side borders.
• 2 (3½" x 78½") top and bottom borders.
If you prefer unpieced borders, cut 4 (3½"-wide) strips lengthwise from alternate yardage and trim to size.

From red print, cut:

• 4 (6½"-wide) lengthwise strips for outer border. Cut strips into:

• 2 (6½" x 86½") side borders.
• 2 (6½" x 90½") top and bottom borders.
• 4 (2¼"-wide) lengthwise strips for binding.

Block Assembly

1. Align corner of appliqué with corner of block. Baste in place within seam allowance. Appliqué, using blanket stitch on curved edge only.
2. Make 90 Daisy Fan blocks.

Quilt Assembly

1. Referring to photo, arrange blocks in 10 horizontal rows of 9 blocks each. Join into rows; join rows to complete center.
2. Measure to ensure that borders will fit. Join 3½" x 80½" pink borders to sides and 3½" x 78½" pink borders to top and bottom.

3. Join 2 (6½" x 86½") red print borders to quilt sides and 2 (6½" x 90½") borders to top and bottom.

Quilting and Finishing

1. Divide backing fabric into 3 (2¾ -yard) lengths. Cut 1 piece in half lengthwise. Sew 1 narrow panel between wide panels. Press seam allowances toward narrow panels. Remaining narrow panel is extra. Seams will run horizontally.

2. Layer backing, batting, and quilt top; baste. Quilt as desired. Quilt shown was outline-quilted in appliqué areas with horizontal lines in block backgrounds. Pink border has 2 lines quilted though it, and outer border has outward repeated lines.

3. Join 2¼"-wide red print strips into 1 continuous piece for straight-grain French-fold binding. Add binding to quilt.

Daisy Fan
BLOCK BY BLOCK
Instructions for 1 (8")
Daisy Fan Block

MATERIALS
1 (8½") square white
1 (8") square print

CUTTING
From print, cut:
• 4 As.

BLOCK ASSEMBLY
1. Align corner of appliqué with corner of block. Baste in place within seam allowance. Appliqué, using blanket stitch on curved edge only.

2. Block should measure 8½". Sign and embroider name in center.

Block Diagram

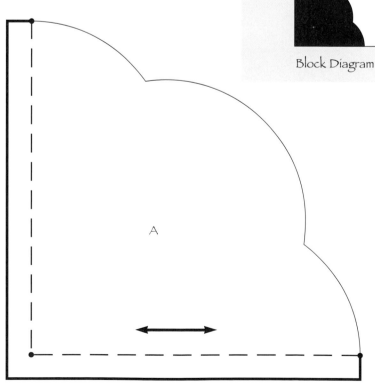

A

Album of Memories
Quilting Pattern

Above, you'll find a fleur-de-lis quilting pattern Alvina Nelson used in her quilt, featured on page 32. "Until recently, I had the pattern I used for quilting," says Alvina Nelson. "Since it was cardboard, I discarded it. The design for the setting blocks was cut from plastic, and I saved it."

Busy as a Bee

If you're part of a small quilting bee, make a group quilt. If each person makes 12 (or desired number) of blocks in her fabrics and signs her name, members can swap with each other at the next gathering. This quilt was made by Rhonda Richards (with help from her bee friends) and quilted by New Traditions.

Busy as a Bee

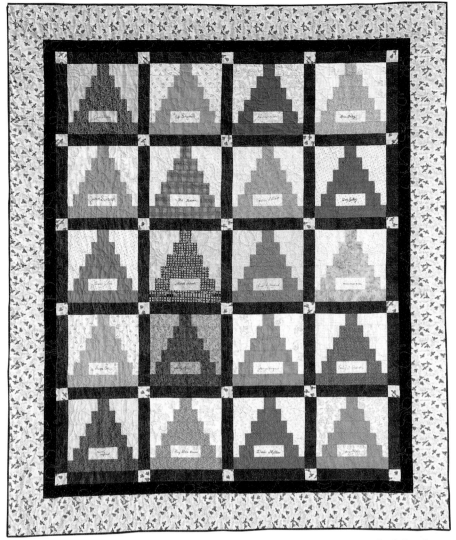

Finished Size: 74" x 88"
Blocks: 20 (12") Beehive Blocks

Materials
20 (2½"-wide) assorted tan strips
20 (2½"-wide) assorted brown
and gold strips
1½ yards brown print for sashing
2¼ yards brown-and-black print
for inner border and binding
2¼ yards bee print for outer border and sashing squares
5½ yards fabric for backing
Full-size batting

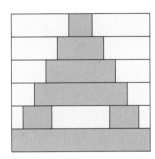

Block Diagram

Cutting
Measurements include ¼" seam
allowances. Border strips are exact
length needed. You may want to
cut them longer to allow for piecing variations. Cut fabric selvage to
selvage unless otherwise noted.

From each tan strip, cut:
- 3 (2½" x 5½") pieces (2 Bs, I).
- 2 (2½" x 4½") pieces (D).
- 2 (2½" x 3½") pieces (F).
- 2 (2½") squares (H).
- 2 (1½" x 2½") pieces (K).

From each brown or gold strip, cut:
- 1 (2½" x 12½") piece (L).
- 1 (2½" x 8½") piece (G).
- 1 (2½" x 6½") piece (E).
- 1 (2½" x 4½") piece (C).

If you have a lot of beginners in your quilting circle, this pattern is ideal for them. All the shapes are simple squares and rectangles—there are no triangles or odd shapes to piece.

- 2 (2½" x 3") pieces (J).
- 1 (2½") square (A).

From brown print, cut:
- 17 (2½"-wide) strips. Cut strips into 49 (2½" x 12½") sashing strips.

From brown-and-black print, cut:
- 4 (2½"-wide) lengthwise strips for inner border. Cut strips into 2 (2½" x 72½") side bor-ders and 2 (2½" x 62½") top and bottom borders.

- 4 (2¼"-wide) lengthwise strips for binding.

From bee print, cut:
- 4 (6½"-wide) lengthwise strips for outer border. Cut strips into 2 (6½" x 76½") side bor-ders and 2 (6½" x 74½") top and bottom borders.
- From remainder, cut 5 (2½"-wide) strips from cut edge to selvage. Cut strips into 30 (2½") sashing squares.

Busy as a Bee

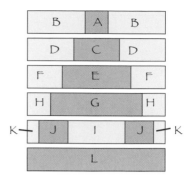

Block Assembly Diagram

Block Assembly

1. Collect signatures on I pieces.
2. Lay out pieces as shown in *Block Assembly Diagram*.
3. Join into horizontal rows; join rows to complete block (*Block Diagram*).
4. Make 20 Beehive blocks.

Quilt Assembly

1. Using photo as a guide, arrange blocks in 5 horizontal rows of 4 blocks each.
2. Join 5 sashing strips and 4 blocks as shown in *Block Row Diagram*. Make 5 block rows.
3. Join 5 sashing squares and 4 sashing strips as shown in *Sashing Row Diagram*. Make 6 sashing rows.
4. Join rows to complete inner quilt top.

5. Add 2½" x 72½" black-and-brown borders to quilt sides. Add 2½" x 62½" black-and-brown borders to quilt top and bottom.
6. Add 6½" x 76½" bee print borders to quilt sides. Add 6½" x 74½" bee print borders to quilt top and bottom.

Quilting and Finishing

1. Divide backing fabric into 2 (2¾-yard) lengths. Cut 1 piece in half lengthwise. Join 1 narrow panel to each side of wide panel. Press seam allowances to narrow panels.
2. Layer backing, batting, and quilt top; baste. Quilt as desired. Quilt shown was machine-quilted with bees all over.
3. Join 2¼"-wide black-and-brown print strips into 1 continuous piece for straight-grain French-fold binding. Add binding to quilt.

Susan McKelvey made the bee stamps used to make this quilt label. For ordering information, see Resources on page 160. For stamping instructions, see page 149.

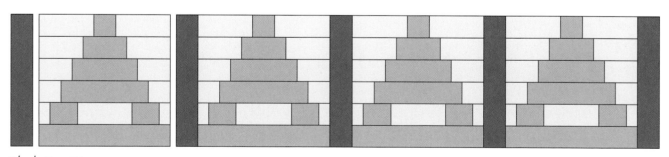

Block Row Diagram

Sashing Row Diagram

Busy as a Bee
BLOCK BY BLOCK

Instructions for 1 (12")
Beehive Block

MATERIALS
1 (2½" x 42") tan strip
1 (2½" x 42") brown or gold strip

CUTTING
From tan strip, cut:
- 3 (2½" x 5½") pieces (2 Bs, I).
- 2 (2½" x 4½") pieces (D).
- 2 (2½" x 3½") pieces (F).
- 2 (2½") squares (H).
- 2 (1½" x 2½") pieces (K).

From brown or gold strip, cut:
- 1 (2½" x 12½") piece (L).
- 1 (2½" x 8½") piece (G).
- 1 (2½" x 6½") piece (E).
- 1 (2½" x 4½") piece (C).
- 2 (2½" x 3") pieces (J).
- 1 (2½") square (A).

BLOCK ASSEMBLY
1. Lay out pieces as shown in *Block Assembly Diagram*.
2. Join into horizontal rows; join rows to complete block (*Block Diagram*). Block should measure 12½". Sign block.

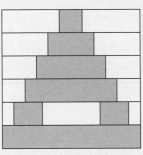

Block Diagram

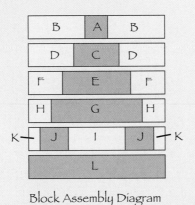

Block Assembly Diagram

The Lord is good, a stronghold in the day of trouble;
And He knows those who trust in Him.

—Nahum 1:7 (NKJV)

Indian Hatchet

Indian Hatchet is perhaps the easiest of all signature blocks. Using the diagonal seams method makes it even faster. We found many examples of this quilt block, all with different interpretations. In the next few pages, you'll see what some quilters have done with this simple block.

General Instructions for Indian Hatchet

Different Sizes, Same Technique

Regardless of the block size you choose, the technique is the same for making Indian Hatchet.

The following instructions are for using the diagonal seams method to make the block. This technique was used on all the quilts in this section.

If you don't want to figure yardage for your own quilt, we've given full instructions for the quilts in the following pages.

Diagonal Seams Method

1. Place small square in upper left corner of background block with right sides facing. Stitch diagonally as shown in *Diagram 1*.

2. Trim ¼" from stitching line (*Diagram 2*).

3. Press open so that seam allowance is behind triangle (*Diagram 3*).

4. Place remaining small square in lower right corner of background block. Stitch diagonally as shown in *Diagram 4*.

5. Trim ¼" from stitching line (*Diagram 5*).

6. Press open to reveal finished block (*Diagram 6*).

.

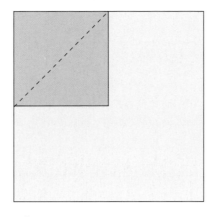

Diagram 1

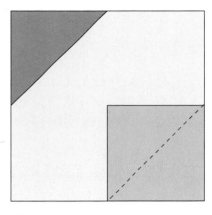

Diagram 4

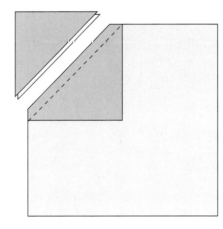

Diagram 2

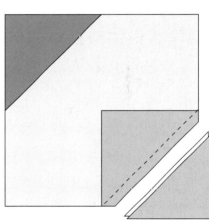

Diagram 5

Diagram 3

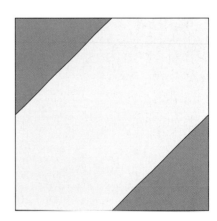

Diagram 6

Butler Family Quilt

Barbara Butler, of Marietta, Georgia, made this signature quilt to document the 96 members of her husband's family. She sent family members packets with blocks, a permanent-ink pen, and instructions for signing the blocks. Barbara finished the quilt just in time for a reunion. "We enjoyed watching everyone find their names and recall memories of the past," says Barbara. "One of my favorite reunion memories was seeing Mrs. Butler look happily at her growing family, turn to Mr. Butler and say, 'Just look what we started!'"

Butler Family Quilt

Finished Size: 66" x 88"
Blocks: 96 (5½") Indian Hatchet
Blocks

Materials

2¾ yards mottled green for
  background
1¼ yards total assorted greens for
  blocks
1¼ yards total assorted browns
  for blocks
¾ yard brown check for inner
  border (2¼ yards for unpieced
  borders)
7¾ yards green check for border,
  backing, and binding
Twin-size batting

Block Diagram

Cutting

Measurements include ¼" seam
allowances. Border strips are exact
length needed. Cut fabric selvage to
selvage unless otherwise noted.

From mottled green, cut:
• 14 (6"-wide) strips. Cut strips
  into 96 (6") squares.
• 4 (3¼") squares for pieced
  border corners.

From assorted greens, cut:
• 96 (4") squares.

From assorted browns, cut:
• 96 (4") squares.

Barbara Butler came up with a clever way to make the half-square triangles used in the pieced border. She simply saved what she trimmed from the blocks, using the diagonal seams method!

Quilt Top Assembly Diagram

From brown check, cut:
• 6 (3¼"-wide) strips. Piece to
  make 2 (3¼" x 44½") inner
  top and bottom borders and 2
  (3¼" x 72") inner side borders.

If you prefer unpieced borders,
cut 4 (3¼"-wide) lengthwise
strips from alternate yardage
and proceed.

Butler Family Quilt

From green check, cut:
- 5½ yards for backing.
- 2¼ yards. Cut yardage into 4 (6"-wide) lengthwise strips for outer border.
- 4 (2¼"-wide) lengthwise strips for binding.

Block Assembly

1. Draw a diagonal line on wrong side of 4" square (Photo A).

2. Place 4" square on corner of 1 (6") square as shown, right sides facing and aligning corners. Stitch along diagonal of 4" square (Photo B).

3. Trim ¼" away from stitching (Photo C).

4. Keep cut triangles together and stitch ¼" from edge (Photo D). Press open.

5. Repeat on opposite corner of 6" square (Photo E).

6. Finished Indian Hatchet block will look like Photo F. Repeat to make 96 blocks, each with 1 green and 1 brown corner. Small triangle squares will be used later in pieced border (Photo G).

Border Assembly

1. Referring to *Quilt Top Assembly Diagram*, join half-square triangle blocks into 4 strips of 13 units and 4 strips of 9 units as shown.

2. Set pieced borders aside.

Quilt Assembly

1. Arrange blocks in 8 horizontal rows of 12 blocks each so that green and brown corners of blocks form green and brown concentric diamonds (*Quilt Top Assembly Diagram*). Join into rows; join rows.

2. Measure width of quilt. Trim 2 brown check borders to size. Join to top and bottom of quilt. Measure length of quilt including

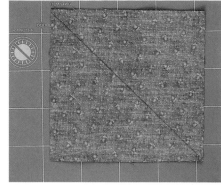

Photo A

Photo D

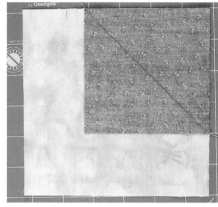

Photo B

Photo E

Photo C

Photo F

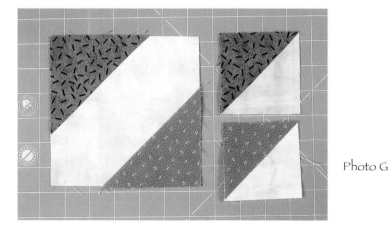

Photo G

Butler Family Quilt

BLOCK BY BLOCK

Instructions for 1 (5½")
Indian Hatchet Block

MATERIALS

1 (6") square mottled green
1 (4") square each green and brown

BLOCK ASSEMBLY

1. Using diagonal seams method, place 1 (4") square on corner of 6" square, right sides facing and aligning corners. Stitch along diagonal of 4" square. Trim ¼" away from stitching. Keep cut triangles together and stitch ¼" from edge. Press open. Repeat on opposite corner of large square.
2. Block should measure 6". Sign block.

Block Diagram

borders. Trim remaining brown check side borders to size and add to opposite sides of quilt top. Press seam allowances toward borders.
3. Join 2 (13-block) border strips as shown. Repeat for opposite side. Join to sides of quilt.
4. Join 2 (9-block) border strips as shown. Add 1 (3¼") green square to each end. Add to top of quilt. Repeat for bottom border.
5. Measure length of quilt. Trim green check side borders to size and add to opposite sides of quilt top. Press seam allowances toward

borders. Measure width of quilt, including borders. Trim remaining 2 green check borders to size. Join to top and bottom of quilt.

Quilting and Finishing

1. Divide backing fabric into 2 (2¾-yard) lengths. Join along sides to make backing.
2. Layer backing, batting, and quilt top; baste. Quilt as desired. Quilt shown was outline-quilted in blocks with center line through signature area. Pieced border was outline-quilted, with design

extended into outer border. Inner border was quilted in half-square triangles.
3. Join 2¼"-wide green check strips into 1 continuous piece for straight-grain French-fold binding. Add binding to quilt.

Love's Celebration

Carolyn Edwards, of Prescott Valley, Arizona, made this quilt for her in-laws' 50th wedding anniversary. She distributed 180 muslin squares reinforced with freezer paper to friends and family to autograph. "It would have been very advantageous to have been able to 'steal' addresses out of Mom's address book, but at the time they lived in Arizona and we lived in Iowa," Carolyn says. "I resorted to seeking the help of family friends." After collecting all of the blocks, arranging them, appliquéing a vine design on the border, and hand-quilting it, Carolyn gave the quilt to her parents-in-law just in time for their 54th wedding anniversary.

Love's Celebration

Finished Size: 64" x 64"
Blocks: 180 (4") Indian Hatchet
Blocks

Materials

1 fat quarter (18" x 22") green
print #1 for bias wreath
1 yard green print #2 for border
bias vines
¼ yard total assorted green prints
for leaves
½ yard total assorted prints for
hearts
1½ yards total assorted pinks for
blocks
1½ yards total assorted blues for
blocks
8½ yards muslin for blocks,
border, backing, and binding
Twin-size batting

Cutting

Measurements include ¼" seam
allowances. Border strips are exact
length needed. You may want to
cut them longer to allow for piecing variations. Cut fabric selvage to
selvage unless otherwise noted.

From green print #1, cut:
• 50" of 1½"-wide bias. Fold and
press to make 50" of ½"-wide
bias for medallion wreath.

From green print #2, cut:
• 300" of 1⅛"-wide bias. Fold
and press to make 300" of ⅜"-
wide bias for border vine.

From assorted green prints, cut:
• 59 leaves, using pattern on
page 84.

From assorted prints, cut:
• 36 hearts in assorted sizes and
shapes (some sample patterns
on page 84).

Elegant appliqué work adds extra beauty to the humble Indian Hatchet block.

From assorted pinks, cut:
• 180 (3") squares.

From assorted blues, cut:
• 180 (3") squares.

From muslin, cut:
• 4 yards for backing.
• 1¾ yards. Cut yardage into 4
(4½"-wide) lengthwise strips.
Cut strips into 4 (4½" x 56½")
border strips.
• Cut 1 (16½") square from
remainder for wreath
background.
• Cut remainder into 10 (4½"-
wide) strips. They will be
approximately 24" wide. Cut
strips into 50 (4½") squares.
• 15 (4½"-wide) strips. Cut strips

into 134 (4½") squares. You
will need a total of 184 (4½")
squares.
• 7 (2¼"-wide) strips for
binding.

Medallion Block Assembly

On 16½" muslin square, appliqué
½"-wide bias in a 12" circle to
make wreath as shown in photo.
Appliqué 7 hearts and 7 leaves
inside circle. Appliqué 9 hearts and
9 leaves outside circle.

Love's Celebration

Hearts

Patterns shown are finished size. Add seam allowance as you cut fabric.

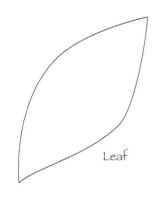

Leaf

Quilt Top Assembly Diagram

Block Assembly

1. Using diagonal seams method and referring to instructions on page 77, place 1 (3") pink square on corner of 1 (4½") square, right sides facing, aligning corners. Stitch along diagonal of 3" square. Trim ¼" away from stitching. Repeat on opposite corner of 4½" square with blue 3" square.

2. Make 180 Indian Hatchet blocks.

Quilt Assembly

1. Lay out medallion block and Indian Hatchet blocks as shown in *Quilt Top Assembly Diagram* to form concentric pink and blue diamonds. Join blocks in each section into rows; join rows to complete each section. Join side sections to medallion block. Add top and bottom sections to complete center.

2. Add 1 (4½" x 56½") border to opposite sides of quilt. Add 1 (4½") square to each end of remaining border strips. Add to top and bottom of quilt.

3. Appliqué ³⁄₈"-wide green print bias vine onto border as shown in photo. Appliqué 20 assorted hearts and 43 leaves.

Quilting and Finishing

1. Divide backing fabric into 2 (2-yard) lengths. Join along sides to make backing.

2. Layer backing, batting, and quilt top; baste. Quilt as desired. Quilt shown was quilted diagonally through Indian Hatchet blocks and outline-quilted around appliqué. Medallion has hearts in corners; borders have diagonal fill in background.

3. Join 2¼"-wide muslin strips into 1 continuous piece for straight-grain French-fold binding. Add binding to quilt.

SIGNATURE QUILT PREPARATION

Carolyn Edwards learned how much preparation is involved in organizing a signature quilt. "About a year before my in-laws' 50th wedding anniversary, I began to distribute muslin squares," says Carolyn.

"I had the advantage of a summer family reunion, which my in-laws did not attend. There, I solicited many autographs and messages. Then I sent packets of cover letters, Pigma™ pens, and muslin squares to everybody my husband and I could think of and could find addresses for.

"As soon as signed muslin squares and Pigma pens would come back to me, I'd put the pens back in the mail the next day with more muslin squares headed in a different direction. It was important to keep notes of where I'd sent squares and when. I started keeping a log of all activity that took place during this quiltmaking process. I now regret not keeping up with that journal."

Love's Celebration
BLOCK BY BLOCK

Instructions for 1 (4")
Indian Hatchet Block

MATERIALS
1 (4½") muslin square
1 (3") square each pink and blue print

BLOCK ASSEMBLY
1. Using diagonal seams method, place 1 (3") square on corner of 4½" square, right sides facing, aligning corners. Stitch along diagonal of 3" square. Trim ¼" away from stitching. Press open.
2. Repeat on opposite corner of 4½" square with blue 3" square. Block should measure 4½". Sign block.

And now abide faith, hope, love, these three; but the greatest of these is love.

—*1 Corinthians 13:13 (NKJV)*

Tennessee Reunion Quilt

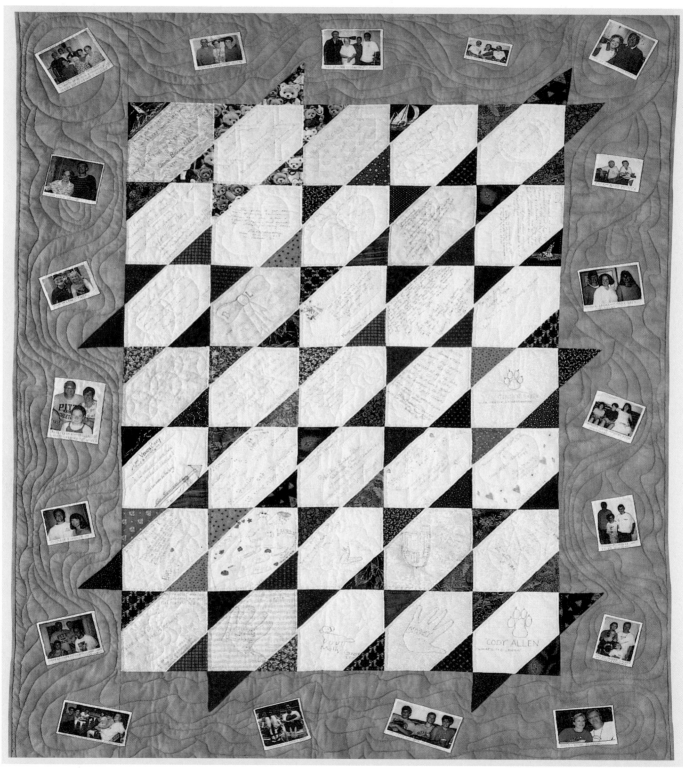

Ann Allen of Westerville, Ohio, made this quilt for her brother and his wife as a thank-you for always hosting their family's reunion. Ann brought white blocks to one of the reunions for family members (ages 6 to 80) to sign. "It was interesting to see how many thought about what they wanted to write or draw long before they sat down to do it," says Ann. "Once I got home, I added colored corners to the blocks and arranged them from top to bottom in descending order of the participants' ages." Ann transferred photographs taken at the reunion to fabric and appliquéd them to the border. She hand-quilted a swirl design in the blue border to depict the lake where the reunion is held. On other parts, Ann quilted designs following what her family members had drawn on the blocks.

Finished Size: 59½" x 75½"
Blocks: 35 (8") Indian Hatchet
Blocks

Materials

2 yards total assorted light prints
1½ yards total assorted dark
   prints (red, green, blue, purple, novelty prints)
2½ yards blue print for border
   and binding
4½ yards white fabric for backing
Twin-size batting
Photo transfers (See page 135.)

Cutting

Measurements include ¼" seam
allowances. Cut fabric selvage to
selvage unless otherwise noted.

From assorted light prints, cut:
• 35 (8½") squares.

From assorted dark prints, cut:
• 79 (4½") squares. Cut at least 6
  squares in each color family.

From blue, cut:
• 3 (10¼"-wide) lengthwise
  strips. Cut strips into 2 (10¼"
  x 76") side border strips and 2
  (10¼" x 40½") top and bottom
  border strips.
• 4 (2¼"-wide) lengthwise strips
  for binding.

Block Assembly

1. Plan corner colors as shown in
photo so that stretched stars are
formed when blocks are joined.
2. Using diagonal seams method
(see page 77), place 1 (4½") dark
square on corner of 1 (8½") light
square, right sides facing and
aligning corners. Stitch along diagonal of dark square. Trim ¼" away
from stitching. Repeat on opposite

corner of light square.
3. Make 35 Indian Hatchet blocks.

Quilt Assembly

1. Lay out blocks in 7 horizontal
rows of 5 blocks each so that
stretched stars are formed by corner colors. Join into rows; join
rows to complete center.
2. Measure to ensure that borders
will fit. Join 2 (10¼" x 40½") top
and bottom borders to quilt. Add
2 (10¼" x 76") side borders to
quilt.
3. Appliqué triangles to border as
shown in photo. Appliqué photo
transfers to border as shown. (See
page 135 for photo transfer
instructions.)

Quilting and Finishing

1. Divide backing fabric into 2
(2¼-yard) lengths. Join along sides
to make backing.
2. Layer backing, batting, and quilt
top; baste. Quilt as desired. Quilt
shown was outline-quilted in
blocks and triangles. Centers of
blocks are quilted in various patterns, such as hand prints, hearts,
paw prints, stars, and bows.
Border is quilted in abstract water
patterns, flowing around photos.
3. Join 2¼"-wide blue strips into 1
continuous piece for straight-grain
French-fold binding. Add binding
to quilt.

Tennessee Reunion

BLOCK BY BLOCK
*Instructions for 1 (8")
Indian Hatchet Block*

Block Diagram

MATERIALS
1 (8½") light square
2 (4½") dark squares

BLOCK ASSEMBLY
1. Using diagonal seams
method, place 1 (4½") dark
square on corner of 1 (8½")
light square, right sides facing
and aligning corners. Stitch
along diagonal of dark square.
Trim ¼" away from stitching.
Repeat on opposite corner of
light square.
2. Block should measure 8½".
Sign block.

Quilt Show Memories

In appreciation of her organizing the quilt show for the Birmingham Quilters' Guild, members made signature blocks for Roxie Elliott of Trussville, Alabama. To further commemorate the event, Roxie added a guild T-shirt to the middle and some photo transfer blocks showing people setting up the show. Notice how turning the blocks in different directions creates a lattice look.

Quilt Show Memories

Finished Size: 50" x 55"
Blocks: 54 (5") Indian Hatchet
Blocks

Materials

1¾ yards total assorted prints for
    blocks
1½ yards muslin
1¼ yards blue batik print for
    border and binding (1¾ yards
    for unpieced borders)
3½ yards muslin backing
11 (5½") photo transfer blocks*
1 guild T-shirt
Twin-size batting
*You do not have to use photo transfer
blocks. Simply make 12 more signature blocks to complete the lattice look.

Cutting

Measurements include ¼" seam
allowances. Border strips are exact
length needed. You may want to
cut them longer to allow for piecing variations. Cut fabric selvage to
selvage unless otherwise noted.

From assorted prints, cut:
• 108 (4½") squares in sets of 2.

From muslin, cut:
• 8 (5½"-wide) strips. Cut strips
   into 55 (5½") squares.

From blue batik print, cut:
• 5 (5½"-wide) strips. Piece as
   necessary to make 2 (5½" x
   40½") top and bottom borders
   and 2 (5½" x 55½") side borders. If you prefer unpieced
   borders, cut 4 (5½"-wide)
   lengthwise strips from alternate
   yardage and trim to size.
   (Binding will be cut lengthwise
   also, in this case.)
• 6 (2¼"-wide) strips for binding.

From T-shirt, cut:
• 1 (10½" x 15½") center block
   (see page 129).

Block Assembly

1. Referring to diagonal seams
method on page 77, place 1 (4½")
square on corner of 5½" square,
right sides facing and aligning corners. Stitch along diagonal of 4½"
square. Trim ¼" away from stitching and press open. Repeat on
opposite corner of muslin square.
2. Make 54 Indian Hatchet blocks.
Remaining muslin square is for signature block.

Quilt Assembly

1. Lay out blocks, photo transfer
blocks*, muslin signature block,
and T-shirt block as shown in *Quilt
Top Assembly Diagram*. Join into
rows; join rows to make sections.

Join side sections to T-shirt block.
Join top and bottom sections to
center.
2. Add blue batik borders to top
and bottom of quilt. Add blue borders to sides of quilt.

Quilting and Finishing

1. Divide backing fabric into 2
(1¾-yard) lengths. Cut 1 piece in
half lengthwise. Sew 1 narrow
panel to 1 side of wide panel. Press
seam allowances toward narrow
panel. Remaining panel is extra.
2. Layer backing, batting, and quilt
top; baste. Quilt as desired. Quilt
shown was quilted in-the-ditch in
blocks, and features a rope pattern
in border.
3. Join 2¼"-wide blue strips into 1
continuous piece for straight-grain
French-fold binding. Add binding
to quilt.

Quilt Top Assembly Diagram

Anderson Family Quilt

Shirley L. Anderson of Republic, Missouri, made this quilt in honor of her husband's family. "They are such a large, close-knit family with an interesting history," says Shirley, "I chose to cover only the offspring of Gustav and Helga Anderson, my husband's parents." The project was quilted by Sue Rasmussen.

Anderson Family Quilt

Finished Size: 64½" x 64½"
Blocks: 64 (6") Lattice Blocks

Materials
2 yards cream-and-red ticking
3 yards total assorted prints
2 yards solid navy
2 yards blue print
4 yards fabric for backing
Twin-size batting

Block Diagram

Cutting
Measurements include ¼" seam allowances. Border strips are exact length needed. You may want to cut them longer to allow for piecing variations. Cut fabric selvage to selvage unless otherwise noted.

From cream-and-red ticking, cut:
- 4 (2¾"-wide) lengthwise strips for border.
- Remainder is approximately 31" wide. Cut remainder into 8 (2¾"-wide) lengthwise strips. Cut strips into 64 (2¾" x 9") rectangles for block signature strip. When cutting strips, consistently align 1 edge of strip with 1 stripe in fabric so that stripes can be matched between blocks.

From assorted prints, cut:
- 64 (5⅜") squares.

- 128 (4⅛") squares.

From solid navy, cut:
- 4 (1½"-wide) lengthwise strips for border.
- 8 (2¼"-wide) crosswise strips from remainder or 4 (2¼"-wide) lengthwise strips for binding.

From blue print, cut:
- 4 (5½"-wide) lengthwise strips for border.

Block Assembly
1. Choose 1 (5⅜") square and 2 (4⅛") squares. Using diagonal seams method and referring to Diagram 1, place 1 (4⅛") square on corner of 1 (5⅜") square, right sides facing and aligning corners.

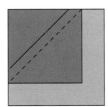

Diagram 1

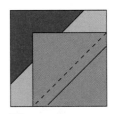

Diagram 2

Diagram 3

Stitch along diagonal of 4⅛" square. Trim ¼" away from stitching. Repeat on opposite corner of 5⅜" square, as shown in Diagram 2. Block should measure 5⅜" square (Diagram 3).
2. Cut block in half diagonally, as shown in Diagram 4 (next page), to make 2 half-square triangles.

Diagram 4

3. Join half-square triangles to opposite sides of 1 (2¾" x 9") stripe rectangle (*Diagram 5*). Square

Diagram 5

Diagram 6

block to 6½" (*Diagram 6*).
4. Make 64 Lattice blocks.

Quilt Assembly

1. Lay out blocks in 8 horizontal rows of 8 blocks each as shown in *Row Assembly Diagram*. Join into rows, turning as needed to form lattice. Referring to photo, join rows to complete center,
2. Join 1 cream-and-red border, 1 navy border, and 1 blue border along sides to make 1 border set. Make 4 border sets.
3. Center border sets on sides of quilt and add, mitering corners.

When the Back Is as Interesting as the Front

Using her computer to make the quilt label (see page 150 for instructions), Shirley Anderson printed a brief history of the Gustav and Helga Anderson family on the quilt label. She pieced the backing, including family photos (see page 135 for photo transfer instructions).

Helga Anderson died on January 17, 1994, at age 93. Her signature is included in the quilt, although the work was not completed until 1995. By that time, there were many additional spouses and grand-children in the family to include.

"I am the current owner of the quilt," says Shirley, "but I plan to pass it along to my daughter, Susan Anderson Saunders."

Row Assembly Diagram

Quilting and Finishing

1. Divide backing fabric into 2 (2-yard) lengths. Cut 1 piece in half lengthwise. Sew 1 narrow panel to each side of wide panel. Press seam allowances toward narrow panels.
2. Layer back, batting, and quilt top; baste. Quilt as desired. Quilt shown was quilted in figure eights in blocks and meander-quilted in outer border.
3. Join 2¼"-wide navy strips into 1 continuous piece for straight-grain French-fold binding. Add binding to quilt.

Anderson Family Quilt
BLOCK BY BLOCK

Instructions for 1 (6")
Lattice Block

MATERIALS
1 (5³⁄₈") print square
2 (4¹⁄₈") assorted print squares
1 (2³⁄₄" x 9") cream-and-red ticking rectangle

BLOCK ASSEMBLY
1. Using diagonal seams method and referring to *Diagram 1,* place 1 (4¹⁄₈") square on corner of 1 (5³⁄₈") square, right sides facing and aligning corners. Stitch along diagonal of 4¹⁄₈" square. Trim ¼" away from stitching. Repeat on opposite corner of 5³⁄₈" square as shown in *Diagram 2.* Block should measure 5³⁄₈" square (*Diagram 3*).
2. Cut block in half diagonally, as shown in *Diagram 4,* to make 2 half-square triangles.
3. Join half-square triangles to opposite sides of 1 (2³⁄₄" x 9") stripe rectangle (*Diagram 5*). Square block to 6½" (*Diagram 6*). Sign block.

Block Diagram

Block Assembly Diagrams

Diagram 1

Diagram 2

Diagram 3

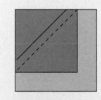

Diagram 4

Diagram 5

Diagram 6

Jacob's Ladder

Darlene Carpenter, of Rodeo, California, found a box of her great-grandmother's quilt squares and fabric in the attic of her grandfather's home. "My mother found blocks that had been made of a dress she had as a little girl and aprons that had been her mother's and grandmother's," she says. Wanting to preserve these blocks, Darlene took a quilting class and learned how to piece the delicate squares together. Once she put the top together and had it machine-quilted, she gave it to her mother for Mother's Day.

Jacob's Ladder

Finished Size: 54" x 54"
Blocks: 36 (9") Jacob's Ladder
Blocks

Materials
36 fat eighths (9" x 22") assorted
   prints
2 yards white
½ yard light print for binding
4 yards muslin for backing
Twin-size batting

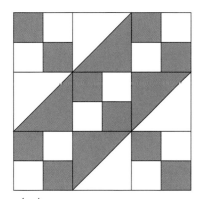

Block Diagram

Cutting
Measurements include ¼" seam
allowances. Border strips are exact
length needed. You may want to
cut them longer to allow for piecing variations. Cut fabric selvage to
selvage unless otherwise noted.

From each assorted print, cut:
- 2 (3⅞") squares. Cut squares in
  half diagonally to make 4 half-
  square triangles (A).
- 10 (2") squares (B).

From white, cut:
- 7 (3⅞"-wide) strips. Cut strips
  into 72 (3⅞") squares. Cut
  squares in half diagonally to
  make 144 half-square triangles
  (A).
- 18 (2"-wide) strips. Cut strips
  into 360 (2") squares (B).

*Darlene Carpenter's grandparents lost part of their home in a fire. "All of my
great-grandmother's quilts were destroyed," says Darlene. "Seven years after the
fire, my grandfather decided to sell the family farm. My mother and I decided to
check the place one more time to see if there was anything left in the attic of
family value. To our surprise, we found a box containing quilt squares and fabric
that had belonged to my great-grandmother, who passed away in 1962. Although
the squares were smoke- and fire-damaged, we were thrilled at this find."*

From light print, cut:
- 6 (2¼"-wide) strips for binding.

Block Assembly
1. Join 1 print A and 1 white A to
make 1 triangle-square as shown in
Diagram 1. Make 4 A squares.
2. Join 1 print B and 1 white B as
shown in *Diagram 2*. Repeat. Join
to make 1 Four-Patch B square.
Make 5 B squares.
3. Lay out squares as shown in
Block Assembly Diagram. Join into
rows; join rows to complete 1

Jacob's Ladder block.
4. Make 36 Jacob's Ladder blocks.

Diagram 1

Diagram 2

Jacob's Ladder

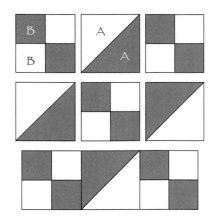

Block Assembly Diagram

Quilt Assembly
1. Arrange blocks in 6 horizontal rows of 6 blocks each as shown in *Quilt Top Assembly Diagram*.
2. Join blocks into rows; join rows.

Quilting and Finishing
1. Divide backing fabric into 2 (2-yard) lengths. Join along sides to make backing.
2. Layer backing, batting, and quilt top; baste. Quilt as desired. Quilt shown was meander-quilted in an allover pattern.
3. Join 2¼"-wide print strips into 1 continuous piece for straight-grain French-fold binding. Add binding to quilt.

Quilt Top Assembly Diagram

THE STORY OF JACOB'S LADDER

Then Jacob departed from Beersheba and went toward Haran. He came to a certain place and spent the night there, because the sun had set; and he took one of the stones of the place and put it under his head, and lay down in that place. He had a dream, and behold, a ladder was set on the earth with its top reaching to heaven; and behold, the angels of God were ascending and descending on it. And behold, the Lord stood above it and said,"I am the Lord, the God of your father Abraham and the God of Isaac; the land on which you lie, I will give it to you and to your descendants. Your descendants will be like the dust of the earth, and you will spread out to the west and to the east and to the north and to the south; and in you and in your descendants shall all the families of the earth be blessed. Behold, I am with you and will keep you wherever you go, and will bring you back to this land; for I will not leave you until I have done what I have promised you." Then Jacob awoke from his sleep and said, "Surely the Lord is in this place, and I did not know it." —*Genesis 28: 10–16 (NASB)*

Jacob's Ladder
BLOCK BY BLOCK

Instructions for 1 (9")
Jacob's Ladder Block

MATERIALS
1 fat eighth (9" x 22") white
1 fat eighth (9" x 22") print

CUTTING
From each, cut:
- 2 (3⅞") squares. Cut squares in half diagonally to make 4 half-square triangles (A).
- 10 (2") squares (B).

BLOCK ASSEMBLY
1. Join 1 print A and 1 white A to make 1 triangle-square as shown in *Diagram 1*. Make 4 A squares.

2. Join 1 print B and 1 white B as shown in *Diagram 2*. Repeat. Join to make 1 Four-Patch B square. Make 5 B squares.

3. Lay out squares as shown in *Block Assembly Diagram*. Join into rows; join rows to complete. Block should measure 9½".

Diagram 1

Diagram 2

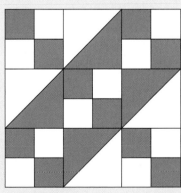

Block Diagram

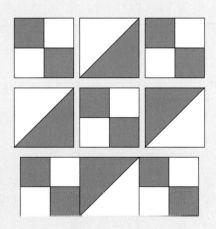

Block Assembly Diagram

Quilter's Pick-Me-Up

In 1993, after a series of stressful events occurred in her life, Laura Edwards, of Knoxville, Tennessee, needed encouragement—and that's just what she got. Friends she met from QuiltNet, an Internet mail list, made floral Nine-Patch blocks and sent them to her. Nine women—two in California plus individuals in Texas, Illinois, New York, and Amsterdam—donated blocks. "They surprised me during a time in my life that I needed a pick-me-up," says Laura. "And it worked!"

Quilter's Pick-Me-Up

Finished Size: 76½" x 86½"
Blocks: 50 (6") Nine-Patch Blocks

Materials

2 yards total assorted floral prints
1 yard marbled green
1 yard solid green
2½ yards solid black
2¼ yards large black floral
5 yards green floral for backing
Full-size batting

Block Diagram

Cutting

Measurements include ¼" seam allowances. Cut fabric selvage to selvage unless otherwise noted.

From assorted floral prints, cut:
• 450 (2½") squares, most in sets of 4 or 5.

From marbled green, cut:
• 20 (1½"-wide) strips. Cut strips into 120 (1½" x 6½") sashing strips.

From solid green, cut:
• 3 (1½"-wide) strips. Cut strips into 71 (1½") sashing squares.
• 2 (11¼"-wide) strips. Cut strips into 5 (11¼") squares. Cut squares in quarters diagonally to make 20 side setting triangles. You will have 2 extra.

Using a multicolored floral print for the border helps unite blocks in a scrap quilt. The floral print also symbolizes a permanent bouquet that Laura Edwards' quilting friends sent her.

• From remainder, cut 2 (6⅝") squares. Cut squares in half diagonally to make 4 corner setting triangles.

From black, cut:
• 4 (1½"-wide) lengthwise strips. Cut strips into 2 (1½" x 62") side borders, 2 (1½" x 73") top and bottom inner borders, and 4 (1½" x 10") top and bottom floral border strips.
• 4 (2½"-wide) lengthwise strips. Cut strips into 2 (2½" x 83") side outer borders and 2 (2½" x 77") top and bottom

outer borders.
• 4 (2¼"-wide) strips for binding.

From large black floral, cut:
• 4 (10"-wide) lengthwise strips. Cut strips into 2 (10" x 62") side borders, 2 (10" x 52") top and bottom borders, and 4 (10") square corners.

Block Assembly

1. Lay out 9 assorted 2½" squares in 3 horizontal rows of 3 squares each (*Block Assembly Diagram*).

Quilter's Pick-Me-Up

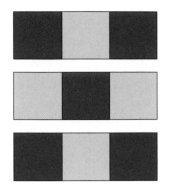

Block Assembly Diagram

Most blocks have 4 or 5 squares that match, but some do not. Join into rows; join rows to make 1 Nine-Patch block (*Block Diagram*).
2. Make 50 Nine-Patch blocks.

Quilt Assembly

1. Referring to *Quilt Top Assembly Diagram*, lay out blocks, sashing strips, and sashing squares as shown. Join into diagonal rows. Add setting triangles to ends of rows. Join rows to complete center.
2. Join 1 (1½" x 62") black side border strip to 1 side of 1 (10" x 62") floral side border. Repeat. Center on each side and join. Trim excess if necessary.
3. Join 1 (1½" x 73") black border strip to top and bottom of quilt.
4. Join 2 (1½" x 10") black border strips, 2 (10") floral squares, and 1 (10" x 52") floral border strip into top border strip as shown. Repeat for bottom border. Add to quilt, matching seams across black 1"-wide border.
5. Measure to ensure that borders will fit. Join 2½" x 83" black borders to quilt sides. Join 2½" x 77" black borders to top and bottom of quilt.

Quilting and Finishing

1. Divide backing fabric into 2 (2½-yard) lengths. Cut 1 piece in half lengthwise. Sew 1 narrow panel to each side of wide panel. Press seam allowances toward narrow panels.
2. Layer backing, batting, and quilt top; baste. Quilt as desired. Quilt shown was quilted in-the-ditch and has meander quilting in border.
3. Join 2¼"-wide black strips into 1 continuous piece for straight-grain French-fold binding. Add binding to quilt.

You can't be brave if you've only had wonderful things happen to you.

—Mary Tyler Moore
(actress)

Quilt Top Assembly Diagram

Quilter's Pick-Me-Up

BLOCK BY BLOCK

Instructions for 1 (6")
Nine-Patch Block

Block Diagram

Block Assembly Diagram

MATERIALS
9 assorted 2½" squares (5 dark and 4 light)

BLOCK ASSEMBLY
1. Lay out 9 assorted 2½" squares in 3 horizontal rows of 3 squares each (*Block Assembly Diagram*). Join into rows; join rows to make 1 Nine-Patch block (*Block Diagram*).

2. Block should measure 6½". Sign block.

Friends and Family Ties

Judie Herzog, of Fairfield, Iowa, and two of her sisters, Carolyn Koopman and Shirley Peterman, pieced this quilt from out-dated ties that belonged to their father and husbands. "As many of our ideas go, the result was bigger than the supply," says Judie. "We had to ask friends to dig into the dark corners of their closets and contribute." Once they assembled the top made of 196 dimensional bow ties, another sister, Erma Kainz, quilted it.

Friends and Family Ties

Finished Size: 84" x 108"
Blocks: 196 (6") Dimensional Bow
Tie Blocks

Materials
196 neckties, seams opened and
　fabric pressed
3½ yards assorted light prints
3 yards blue-and-gold print
8¼ yards muslin for backing
Queen-size batting

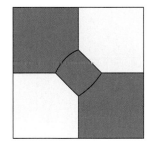

Block Diagram

Cutting
Measurements include ¼" seam
allowances. Cut fabric selvage to
selvage unless otherwise noted.

From each necktie, cut:
• 3 (3½") squares.

From assorted light prints, cut:
• 196 sets of 2 (3½") squares.

From blue-and-gold print, cut:
• 8 (3½"-wide) lengthwise strips
　for borders.
• 4 (2¼"-wide) lengthwise strips
　for binding.

Block Assembly
1. Choose 3 necktie squares and 2
print squares. Fold 1 necktie
square in half, right sides out, to
make 1 (1¾" x 3½") rectangle.
2. Layer rectangle between 1 necktie square and 1 print square, right

Instead of giving Dad another tie this year, make use of his old ones!

sides facing and raw edges aligned.
Stitch across 1 edge as shown in
Diagram 1, page 104, catching
short end of rectangle in seam.
3. Unfold and press both squares
away from rectangle (*Diagram 2*).
4. Repeat Steps 2 and 3 on opposite
end of rectangle, reversing print
and necktie order (*Diagram 3*).
5. Unfold and press both squares
away from rectangle to form a
"bridge" (*Diagram 4*).
6. Open rectangle and refold pieces

as shown in *Diagram 5,* aligning all
raw edges and seam lines. Stitch
top edge, staggering seams
(*Diagram 6*).
7. Press. A three-dimensional Bow
Tie knot is formed by the folded
rectangle (*Diagram 7*).
8. Make 196 Dimensional Bow Tie
blocks.

Quilt Assembly
1. Lay out blocks in 14 horizontal-
rows of 10 blocks each as shown in

photo. Join into rows; join rows to complete center.

2. Measure length of quilt. Trim 2 borders to size and add to opposite sides of quilt top. Press seam allowances toward borders. Measure width of quilt, including borders. Trim 2 borders to size. Join to top and bottom of quilt.

3. Join 15 blocks into a strip. Repeat. Add to sides of quilt.

4. Join 13 blocks into a strip. Repeat. Add to top and bottom of quilt.

5. Add outer border as described in Step 2 above.

Quilting and Finishing

1. Divide backing fabric into 3 (2¾-yard) lengths. Join along sides to make backing. Seams will run horizontally.

2. Layer backing, batting, and quilt top; baste. Quilt as desired. Quilt shown was quilted in an allover looping pattern around center of blocks. Borders feature straight-line quilting.

3. Join 2¼"-wide blue-and-gold print strips into 1 continuous piece for straight-grain French-fold binding. Add binding to quilt.

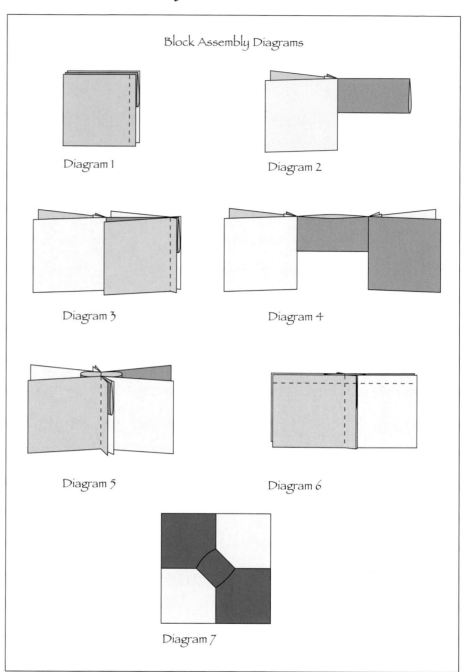

Block Assembly Diagrams

Diagram 1

Diagram 2

Diagram 3

Diagram 4

Diagram 5

Diagram 6

Diagram 7

Honor your father and your mother, so that you may live long in the land the Lord your God is giving you.

—*Exodus 20: 12 (NIV)*

Friends and Family Ties
BLOCK BY BLOCK

*Instructions for 1 (6") Dimensional
Bow Tie Block*

Block Assembly Diagrams

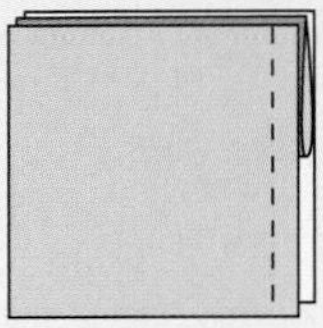

Diagram 1

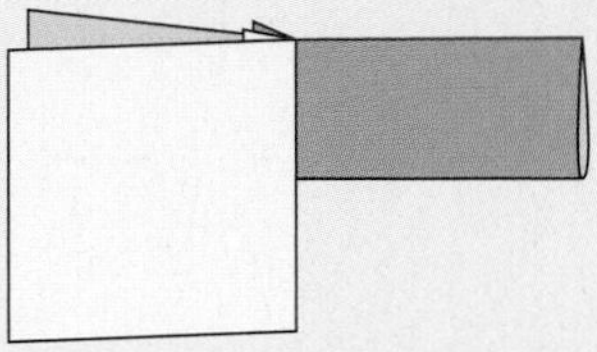

Diagram 2

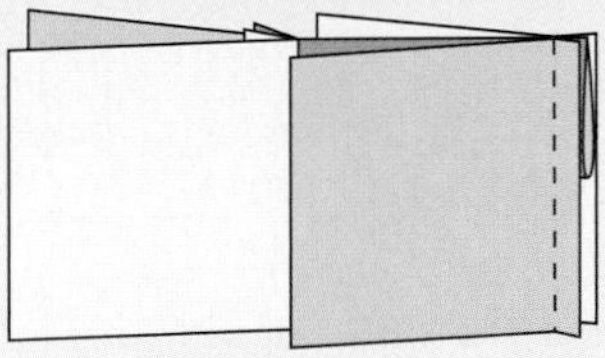

Diagram 3

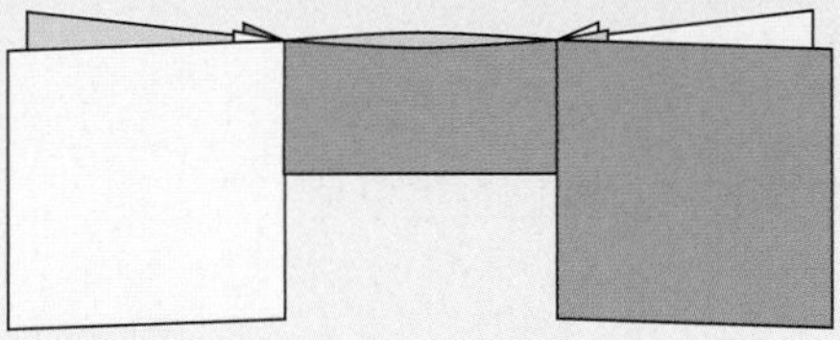

Diagram 4

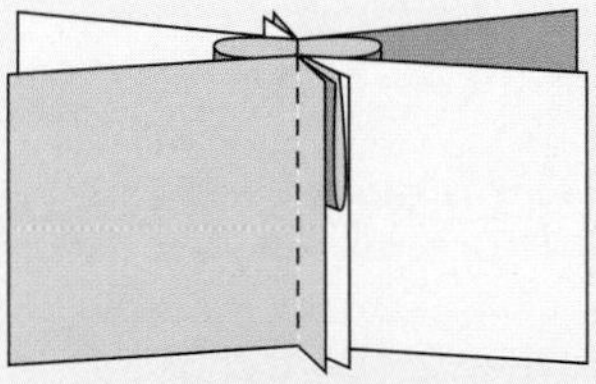

Diagram 5

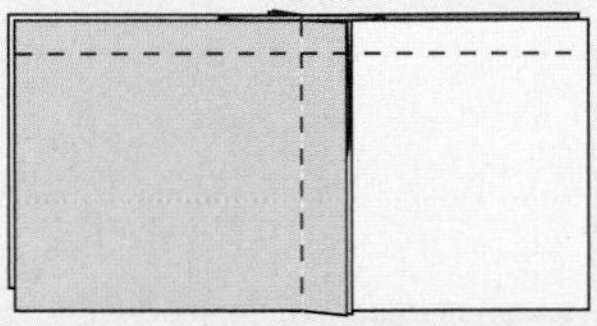

Diagram 6

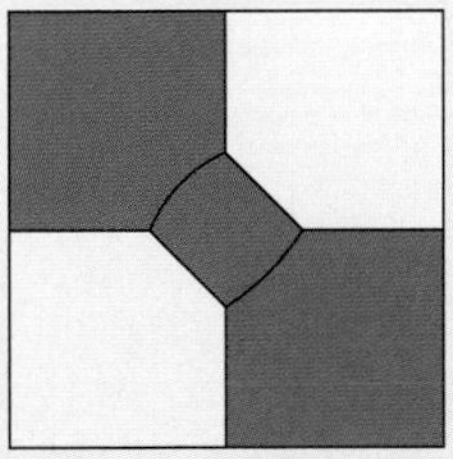

Diagram 7

MATERIALS
3 (3½") necktie squares
2 (3½") print squares

BLOCK ASSEMBLY
1. Fold 1 necktie square in half, right sides out, to make 1 (1¾" x 3½") rectangle.

2. Layer rectangle between 1 necktie square and 1 print square, right sides facing and raw edges aligned. Stitch across 1 edge as shown in *Diagram 1*, catching short end of rectangle in seam.

3. Unfold and press both squares away from rectangle (*Diagram 2*).

4. Repeat Steps 2 and 3 on opposite end of rectangle, reversing print and necktie order (*Diagram 3*).

5. Unfold and press both squares away from rectangle to form a "bridge" (*Diagram 4*).

6. Open rectangle and refold pieces as shown in *Diagram 5*, aligning all raw edges and seam lines. Stitch top edge, staggering seams (*Diagram 6*).

7. Press. A three-dimensional Bow Tie knot is formed by the folded rectangle (*Diagram 7*). Block should measure 6½".

Crow's Feet

"As Mary B. Larson approached her 50th birthday," says Lynn Witzenburg, "we decided to make a quilt for her. Crow's Feet blocks have become the traditional gift among us for 50th birthdays, just as Tree of Life* blocks are for 40th birthdays, because everyone knows 40 isn't old if you're a tree. Each member agreed to make two or more Crow's Feet blocks in Mary B's favorite fabrics: homespun plaids."
*Cardinals in Friendship Pines on page 64 is made using Tree of Life (or Pine Tree) blocks.

Crow's Feet

Finished Size: 74½" x 76½"
Blocks: 36 (6⅞") Crow's Feet
Blocks

Materials
36 assorted fat eighths (9" x 22")
   light prints for blocks
36 assorted fat eighths (9" x 22")
   dark prints for blocks
4 yards brown print for setting
   pieces and pieced borders (5
   yards for unpieced borders)
1¼ yards black for pieced border
   and binding (2 yards for
   unpieced borders)
4¾ yards fabric for backing
Full-size batting

Block Diagram

Members of the Rather Bees quilting bee of Des Moines made Crow's Feet blocks to celebrate the 50th birthday of member Mary B. Larson. They set them together at a party in her honor. Later that day, Mary B. became ill at home. Her heart, damaged by several attacks, was not strong enough to recover. Mary B., beloved by many, passed away. The Rather Bees finished the quilt and gave it to her husband, David, and son, Sean.

Cutting
Measurements include ¼" seam allowances. Cut fabric selvage to selvage unless otherwise noted.

From assorted light prints, cut:
- 36 matching sets of:
  - 9 (1⅞") squares (C).
  - 2 (2⅝") squares. Cut squares in quarters diagonally to make 8 quarter-square triangles (A).

From assorted dark prints, cut:
- 36 matching sets of:
  - 2 (1⅞" x 4⅝") rectangles (D).
  - 2 (1⅞") squares (C).

- 4 (2¼") squares. Cut squares in half diagonally to make 8 half-square triangles (B).
- 2 (2⅝") squares. Cut squares in quarters diagonally to make 8 quarter-square triangles (A).

From brown print, cut:
- 8 (6"-wide) strips. Piece strips to make 2 (6" x 80") top and bottom borders and 2 (6" x 83") side borders. For unpieced borders, cut 4 (6" x 90") lengthwise strips. Trim after adding to quilt and mitering corners.

- 1 (11⅛"-wide) strip. Cut strip into 3 (11⅛") squares. Cut squares in half diagonally to make 6 half-square setting triangles (X).
- 1 (6"-wide) strip. Cut strip into 6 (6") squares. Cut squares in half diagonally to make 12 half-square setting triangles (Y).
- 6 (11½"-wide) strips. Cut strips into 17 (11½") squares. Cut squares in quarters diagonally to make 68 quarter-square setting triangles (Z). You will have 2 extra.

Crow's Feet

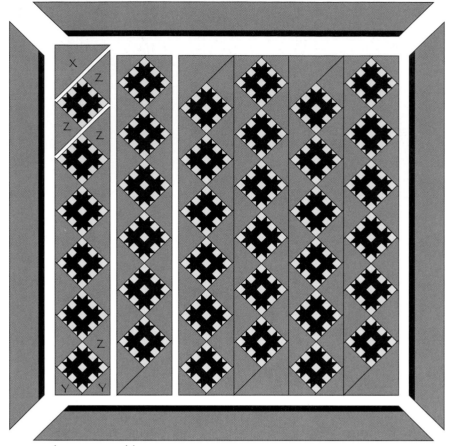

Quilt Top Assembly Diagram

From black, cut:
- 8 (1½"-wide) strips. Piece strips to make 4 (1½" x 72") borders. For unpieced borders, cut 4 (1½" x 72") lengthwise strips. Trim after adding to quilt and mitering corners.
- 8 (2¼"-wide) strips for binding (10 strips if using unpieced border leftovers).

Left Point Unit Diagram

Right Point Unit Diagram

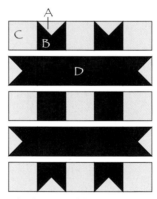

Block Assembly Diagram

Block Assembly

1. Join 1 dark A to 1 light A to make a triangle. Join to a matching dark B triangle to make a square point unit. Make 4 left and 4 right point units as shown in *Point Unit Diagrams*.

2. Lay out 9 light Cs, 2 dark Cs, 2 dark Ds, and 8 point units as shown in *Block Assembly Diagram*. Join into rows; join rows to complete block (*Block Diagram*).

3. Make 36 blocks. For variety, you can make point units from 1 fabric and dark Cs and Ds from another.

Quilt Assembly

1. Referring to *Quilt Top Assembly Diagram,* arrange blocks in 6 columns of 6 blocks as shown.

2. Join 2 Z setting triangles to each side of 30 blocks as shown. *Note: Setting pieces are slightly larger to allow blocks to "float" between columns.* Join 1 Z and 1 Y triangle to sides of 6 blocks as shown. Join blocks in each column of diagonal rows, matching block points. Add X and Y setting triangles to ends of columns.

3. Using long ruler and rotary cutter, trim sides of rows ½" beyond corners of blocks.

4. Join columns.

5. Center and sew black borders to each brown border. Press seam allowance toward brown borders.

Center and sew borders to quilt sides; miter border corners.

Quilting and Finishing

1. Divide backing fabric into 2 (2⅜"-yard) lengths. Cut 1 piece in half lengthwise. Join 1 narrow panel to each side of wide panel. Press seam allowances toward narrow panels.

2. Layer backing, batting, and quilt top; baste. Quilt as desired. Quilt shown was quilted in-the-ditch around dark portion of each block and outline-quilted ¼" inside each block. Setting triangles and borders have a feather pattern.

3. Join 2¼"-wide black strips into 1 continuous piece for French-fold straight-grain binding. Add binding to quilt.

Crow's Feet
BLOCK BY BLOCK

Instructions for 1 (6⅞")
Crow's Feet Block

MATERIALS
1 fat eighth* light print
1 fat eighth* dark print
*Fat eighth – 9" x 22"

CUTTING
From light print, cut:
- 9 (1⅞") squares (C).
- 2 (2⅞") squares. Cut squares in quarters diagonally to make 8 quarter-square triangles (A).

From dark print, cut:
- 2 (1⅞" x 4⅝") rectangles (D).
- 2 (1⅞") squares (C).
- 4 (2¼") squares. Cut squares in half diagonally to make 8 half-square triangles (B).
- 2 (2⅝") squares. Cut squares in quarters diagonally to make 8 quarter-square triangles (A).

BLOCK ASSEMBLY
1. Join 1 dark A to 1 light A to make a triangle. Join to a matching dark B triangle to make a square point unit. Make 4 left and 4 right point units as shown in *Point Unit Diagrams*.

2. Lay out 9 light Cs, 2 dark Cs, 2 dark Ds, and 8 point units as shown in *Block Assembly Diagram*. Join into rows; join rows to complete block (*Block Diagram*). Block should measure 7⅜".

Block Diagram

Left Point Unit Diagram

Right Point Unit Diagram

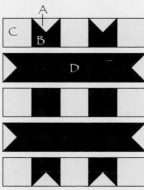

Block Assembly Diagram

Handkerchief and Memorabilia Quilts

Do you have a collection of handkerchiefs handed down to you from your mother or a dear aunt? Or perhaps you collect handkerchiefs from antique shops and thrift stores. Consider making them into an elegant quilt, where you can enjoy the handkerchiefs every day. Think what a wonderful Mother's Day or birthday gift such a quilt would make. You can also embellish the quilt with trinkets, buttons, photo transfer, and other memorabilia.

General Instructions for Handkerchief and Memorabilia Quilts

Preparing Handkerchiefs

Many handkerchiefs have pretty decorative edges. For this reason, you will probably want to appliqué them to a background block rather than sewing them to each other. Most handkerchiefs tend to be lightweight, stretchy, and sheer (Photo A), making them difficult to work with in a quilt project. If you follow the simple steps below, you will find it much easier to appliqué your handkerchiefs.

1. Wash the handkerchiefs gently by hand, one at a time, in warm water, using a mild detergent. Spread on a towel and use your fingers to flatten and to straighten hems.
2. Press. If a handkerchief is excessively limp, spray it lightly with sizing.
3. Because of the differences in size and edgings on handkerchiefs, you will need to mount them on background blocks. Measure the assortment of handkerchiefs you have chosen and determine a block size by adding at least 1½" to the largest measurement. The background fabric will show around each handkerchief. (Many are

Photo A

about 12" square, and a 14" background block works well.)
4. Following manufacturer's instructions, fuse lightweight interfacing to the wrong side of the handkerchief (Photo B). Try to avoid the kind with small dots on the interfacing, as they might show through.

Photo B

Photo C

5. Using small scissors, carefully trim away excess interfacing extending beyond handkerchief (Photo C). Or you may want to cut the interfacing just smaller than the handkerchief and then fuse it.

Photo D

6. The stabilized handkerchief is still lightweight but not as transparent (Photo D).

Adding Buttons

Adding buttons, pins, and small trinkets can add much sentimental value to a quilt. However, these items are often best used on wall hangings or decorative pieces. Never put these items on a baby quilt, to prevent the risk of choking. Use quilting thread or pearl cotton to keep buttons secure.

Adding Memorabilia

Use your imagination when making a memory quilt. Try to personalize it for your recipient. Using photo transfer techniques described on page 135, you can add such items as:

- Wedding or school photos
- Marriage certificates
- Birth certificates
- Report cards
- Letters
- Ribbons or awards
- Newspaper clippings
- Diplomas

Connecting Threads

Carolyn Maruggi, of Pittsford, New York, made this quilt as a tribute to her maternal grandmother, Martha Behling Kohl. Carolyn's mother, Thelma Baumgartner, is the current owner. The quilt exemplifies just about every technique possible in making memory quilts. "Mom adores the quilt," says Carolyn. "Of all the things I've made, this has been one of the most satisfying. Everyone who sees it is reminded of stories, and I like that."

Connecting Threads

There is so much to see in Carolyn Maruggi's quilt, we just couldn't resist showing you close-ups of the many details. Rather than trying to replicate her quilt exactly, we hope that you will use some of her ideas to make your own unique memorabilia quilt.

Finished Size: 34½" x 37½" (excluding prairie points)

Getting Started

"I inherited a small collection of textiles made by my grandmother," says Carolyn. "Then one day, the idea hit me to use the embroidered tablecloth as the quilt's background. It's a wonderful feeling to have an idea hit you out of the blue like that. Since then, I keep an eye out for other suitable linens to use as quilt backgrounds. They are easy to work with, and it's especially nice to know that they don't have to be hidden away in a closet.

"The doilies and yo-yo block were made by my grandmother. The old buttons and lace I had long collected, just waiting for the perfect opportunity to use them."

Photo Transfer

See page 135 for photo transfer instructions.

"Photos are an important part of my family's memories," says Carolyn, "and as family historian, I had many great old pictures from which to choose."

Carolyn made this quilt before photo transfer techniques and materials were widely available. "I had to learn how to do sun prints myself," says Carolyn. "I ordered the chemicals and directions from a local source. I worked in my

Begin with a large vintage linen, like a tablecloth, to use as a foundation for other memorabilia. Appliqué doilies, quilt blocks, and buttons as desired. To personalize the quilt, like this one, add photo transfers and write stories next to important pieces. You can even mix old and new materials.

husband Edward's wine cellar, the darkest room in the house, with a red light. My first attempt turned out too light, but the second set came out perfectly."

Block Diagram

Quilt Blocks

If you have some antique quilt blocks, but not enough to make an actual quilt, consider appliquéing them to a memorabilia quilt. Although Carolyn made these blocks, you can use antique quilt squares in a similar manner.

"Wanting to share the quilt with Mom's family, I knew I needed to incorporate all of her siblings," Carolyn says. "I decided to include their names on eight-pointed stars."

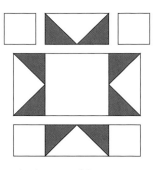

Block Assembly Diagram

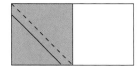

Diagram 1

Diagram 2

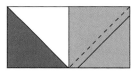

Diagram 3

Diagram 4

Carolyn made blocks for each of her mother's siblings, but you may want to appliqué antique quilt blocks to your piece.

Instructions for 1 (5") Variable Star Block

Materials

1 (3") square muslin for center

4 (1¾" x 3") pieces muslin for star point backgrounds

4 (1¾") squares for background corners

8 (1¾") squares dark print for star points

Block Assembly

1. With wrong sides facing, fold 1¾" dark squares in half diagonally and press a crease.

2. With right sides facing, place 1 dark square atop 1 end of 1¾" x 3" muslin rectangle. Stitch from corner to corner along diagonal crease (*Diagram 1*).

3. Trim the fabric from the diagonal corner fabric only, leaving a ¼" seam allowance. Press triangle back (*Diagram 2*).

4. Place another dark square over other end of rectangle and stitch from corner to corner along crease (*Diagram 3*). Trim and press open (*Diagram 4*).

5. Repeat with remaining pieces to make 4 star point units.

6. Arrange pieces as shown in *Block Assembly Diagram*. Join into rows; join rows to complete block (*Block Diagram*).

Writing

"I hadn't thought of putting the writing on the quilt until I started working on it," admits Carolyn. "I've always driven my family a little bit crazy by bringing out the pencil and paper whenever they started telling stories of the old days. I wanted to write about Mom's life growing up on the farm, and I realized that this quilt would be the perfect place to write at least a little bit of what Mom had told me." See page 149 for information on writing on fabric.

Prairie Points

If you would like to add prairie points to your quilt, follow these instructions:

1. Fold 3¾" squares in half (*Diagram A*); then fold each piece in half again to make a small triangle (*Diagram B*).

2. Arrange prairie points along each side of quilt, with each triangle nesting inside its neighbor as needed to fit (*Diagram C*).

3. Aligning raw edges of triangles and quilt border, space prairie points evenly and baste through top and batting only, keeping backing free.

4. Folding backing out of the way, stitch prairie points in place through top and batting (*Diagram D*).

5. Trim batting even with quilt top. Trim backing 1" larger on all sides. Turn under raw edge of backing, covering raw edges of prairie points, and blindstitch in place (*Diagram E*).

Connecting Threads

Prairie Points Diagrams

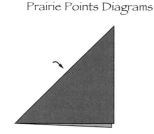

Diagram A

Diagram B

Diagram C

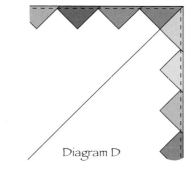

Diagram D

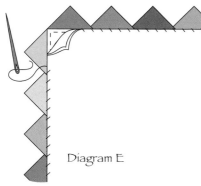

Diagram E

Carolyn found a great photo of her grandmother feeding chickens on the farm. She put some modern ceramic chicken buttons around the photo and wrote beside it, "Grandma was fond of her chickens. She sold butter and eggs for pin money. There was always chicken for Sunday dinner."

Quilt Label

Carolyn made a detailed map of the quilt on a piece of muslin, explaining the origin of all the items on the front of the quilt. She drew a simple outline, numbered the pieces, and wrote a description of each. As the quilt is exhibited in shows or wins awards, Carolyn adds quilt labels so future generations will know the quilt's entire story.

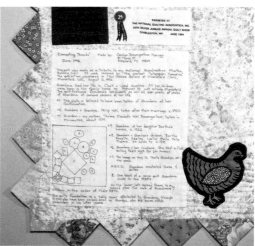

Quilt labels are a vital part of the quilt's history. You can add more quilt labels as the quilt is exhibited or wins awards.

Carolyn included a photo of her grandparents at the top of the quilt and wrote their names and wedding date beside it. Several other photos are included on the quilt.

> *Imagination is the highest kite one can fly.*
>
> —Lauren Bacall (American actress)

Memory Vests

If you have a collection of old handkerchiefs or embroidered pieces, you might consider making them into a vest. The vests on these pages were made by Sharon Morton of North Olmsted, Ohio. "I used linens found at garage sales, flea markets, and antique shops," says Sharon. "My thanks to the unknown women who embroidered them!"

Memory Vests

Materials

Purchased vest pattern

Muslin according to package
yardage

Vintage linens (handkerchiefs,
napkins, dresser scarves, pil-
low case)

Mother of pearl vintage buttons

Assembly

1. Cut out vest pattern, following
pattern instructions.

2. Arrange vintage linens in a
pleasing manner on vest front and
back pieces. Appliqué or machine-
stitch in place. Add buttons as
desired on front. (Don't put buttons on back—they will hurt when
you lean back in a chair.)

3. Finish vest according to pattern
instructions.

Starting Your Collection

If you don't have a
large collection of
linens, you can
combine a few
pieces with tradi-
tional patchwork.
Table scarves
(comparable to
table runners

today) often have the same design repeated at each
end. Sharon found one with baskets and used them to
make this pretty vest.

*Vintage buttons can be decorative, as shown on this vest, or
you can make functional buttons and buttonholes. Don't
worry about finding a matching set of buttons. By mixing
different buttons of similar sizes, you add visual interest.*

*Be creative as you place your vintage pieces. Sharon placed
an attractive pillowcase edge across the bottom of this vest
and used a corner of a table scarf for the upper back.*

Mother's Handkerchiefs

Sharon Newman of Lubbock, Texas, made this quilt in 1992, using her mother's handkerchiefs. Sharon presented the quilt to her daughter, Vicki Lea, as a remembrance of her grandmother, Elsie Lea Hicks.

Mother's Handkerchiefs

Finished Size: 45¾" x 64¼"
Blocks: 8 (13") Blocks

Materials
1¼ yards pale gray (1¾ yards for unpieced borders)
1½ yards pink print
1¼ yards red print for border and binding (1¾ yards for unpieced borders)
4 yards gray print for backing
8 (10" to 12") square handkerchiefs
Twin-size batting

Cutting
Measurements include ¼" seam allowances. Cut fabric selvage to selvage unless otherwise noted.

From pale gray, cut:
- 2 (13½"-wide) strips. Cut strips into 6 (13½") squares.
- 5 (2"-wide) strips. Piece as necessary to make 2 (2" x 55¾") side borders and 2 (2" x 40¼") top and bottom borders.
- Alternate cutting: If you prefer unpieced borders, cut 4 (2"-wide) lengthwise strips from alternate yardage and trim to size. Cut 6 (13½") squares from remainder.

From pink print, cut:
- 1 (13½"-wide) strip. Cut strip into 2 (13½") squares.
- 1 (19¾"-wide) strip. Cut strip into 2 (19¾") squares. Cut squares in quarters diagonally to make 8 side setting triangles. You will have 2 extra.
- 1 (10⅛"-wide) strip. Cut strip into 2 (10⅛") squares. Cut squares in half diagonally to make 4 corner setting triangles.

Remember that you can get more mileage from only a few handkerchiefs if you set the blocks on point.

From red print, cut:
- 6 (3½"-wide) strips. Piece to make 2 (3½" x 58¾") side borders and 2 (3½" x 46¼") top and bottom borders. If you prefer unpieced borders, cut 4 (3½"-wide) lengthwise strips from alternate yardage and trim to size. Binding [4 (2¼"-wide) lengthwise strips] will also be cut lengthwise here.
- 6 (2¼"-wide) strips for binding.

Block Assembly
1. Center 1 handkerchief on 1 (13½") square and appliqué in place.
2. Make 8 Handkerchief blocks.

Quilt Assembly

1. Lay out handkerchief blocks and setting triangles as shown in *Quilt Top Assembly Diagram.* Join into diagonal rows; join rows.
2. Measure to ensure that borders will fit. Join 2 (2" x 55¾") gray borders to quilt sides. Add 2 (2" x 40¼") gray borders to top and bottom of quilt.
3. Join 2 (3½" x 58¾") red borders to quilt sides. Add 2 (3½" x 46¼") red borders to top and bottom of quilt.

Quilting and Finishing

1. Divide backing fabric into 2 (2-yard) lengths. Cut 1 piece in half lengthwise. Sew 1 narrow panel to 1 side of wide panel. Press seam allowances toward narrow panel. Remaining panel is extra and can be used to make hanging sleeve.
2. Layer backing, batting, and quilt top; baste. Quilt as desired. Quilt shown was quilted in-the-ditch around each block and handkerchief. There are feathered hearts in the setting triangles and waves in the gray border.
3. Join 2¼"-wide red print strips into 1 continuous piece for straight-grain French-fold binding. Add binding to quilt.

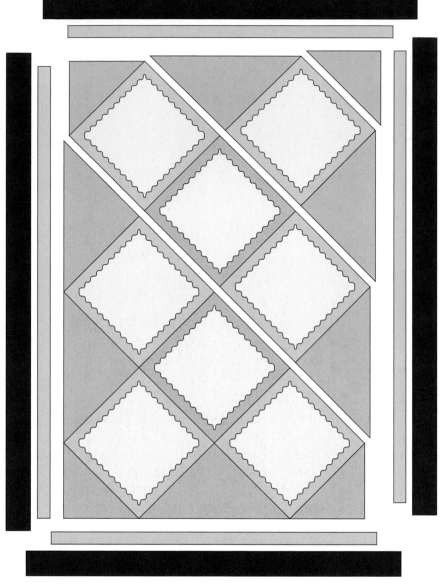

Quilt Top Assembly Diagram

Charm is deceitful and beauty is passing,

but a woman who fears the Lord,

she shall be praised.

—Proverbs 31:30 (NKJV)

Mother's Handkerchiefs

BLOCK BY BLOCK

Instructions for 1 (13")
Handkerchief Block

MATERIALS
1 (13½") gray or pink print square
1 (10" to 12") square handkerchief

BLOCK ASSEMBLY
Center handkerchief on 13½" square and appliqué in place.

Flutterbys

Dorothy Perry of Lubbock, Texas, found a unique way to display her handkerchief collection. Using her most ornate pieces, she folded them into butterflies and stitched them into a quilt.

Flutterbys

Finished Size: 78" x 96¾"
Blocks: 12 (16") Butterfly Blocks

Materials

3 yards white-on-white print for
  block backgrounds
2¼ yards red stripe for sashing
  and border
3 yards solid red for border and
  binding
6 yards pink print for backing
Embroidery floss to match
12 (11" to 13") square handkerchiefs
Queen-size batting

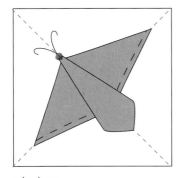

Block Diagram

Cutting

Measurements include ¼" seam
allowances. Cut fabric selvage to
selvage unless otherwise noted.

From white-on-white print, cut:

- 6 (16½"-wide) strips. Cut strips
  into 12 (16½") squares for
  block backgrounds.

From red stripe, cut:

- 8 (3¼"-wide) lengthwise strips,
  centering on stripe. Cut strips
  into 2 (3¼" x 78¼") side borders, 2 (3¼" x 59½") top and
  bottom borders, 2 (3¼" x
  72¾") vertical sashing strips,
  and 9 (3¼" x 16½") horizontal sashing strips.

*If you collect handkerchiefs, look for ones with busy prints or scalloped edges to
make pretty butterflies.*

From solid red, cut:

- 2¼ yards. Cut 4 (10"-wide)
  lengthwise strips. Cut strips
  into 2 (10" x 78¼") side borders and 2 (10" x 78½") top
  and bottom borders.
- 9 (2¼"-wide) strips for binding.

Block Assembly

1. Crease background square diagonally in both directions to make
guidelines (*Diagram 1*).
2. Fold handkerchief diagonally with
top edge slightly over bottom edge.

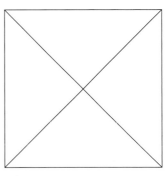

Diagram 1

Pin or baste edges together (*Diagram
2*). Lay handkerchief diagonally on
creased background.

Flutterbys

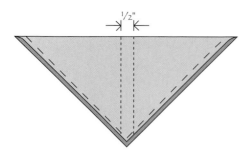

Diagram 2
Back view of handkerchief

3. Fold tuck under on each side of center, leaving ½" at top of fold. Tug gently to form head of butterfly (*Diagram 3*). Both sides of body should have same size tuck, and center of body should be aligned with diagonal of block. Wings should angle away from head and tips should align with opposite diagonal of block (*Block Diagram*).

Diagram 3 (front)

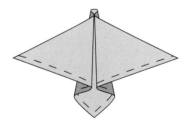

Diagram 4 (back)

4. When satisfied with placement, pin in place. Appliqué to background. Satin-stitch head. Embroider antennae, using *Antennae Pattern*.
5. Make 12 Butterfly Blocks.

Quilt Assembly
1. Referring to photo, alternate 4 blocks and 3 sashing strips. Join into vertical row; make 3 block rows. Join rows with sashing strips to complete center.
2. Add 1 stripe border to each side of quilt. Miter corners.
3. Measure to ensure that borders will fit. Join 2 (10" x 78¼") borders to quilt sides. Join 2 (10" x 78½") borders to top and bottom of quilt.

Quilting and Finishing
1. Divide backing fabric into 2 (3-yard) lengths. Join along sides to make backing.
2. Layer backing, batting, and quilt top; baste. Quilt as desired. Quilt shown was quilted in butterfly area to define wings and by the handkerchief pattern. Background was quilted in leaves and flowers. Sashing has a double wave and border has a butterfly pattern.
3. Join 2¼"-wide red strips into 1 continuous piece for straight-grain French-fold binding. Add binding to quilt.

Butterflies...not quite birds, as they were not quite flowers, mysterious and fascinating as are all indeterminate creatures.

—Elizabeth Goudge
(English novelist)

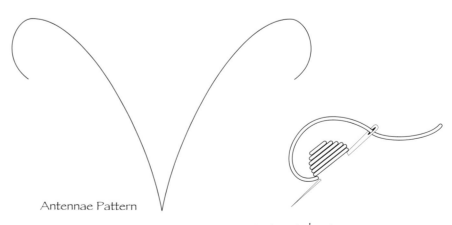

Antennae Pattern

Satin-stitch Diagram

Flutterbys
BLOCK BY BLOCK

Instructions for 1 (16")
Butterfly Block

MATERIALS
1 (16½") white-on-white print square
1 (11" to 13") square handkerchief
Embroidery floss to match

BLOCK ASSEMBLY
1. Crease background square diagonally in both directions to make guidelines (*Diagram 1*).

2. Fold handkerchief in half diagonally with top edge slightly over bottom edge. Pin or baste edges together (*Diagram 2*). Lay handkerchief diagonally on creased background

3. Fold tuck under on each side of center, leaving ½" at top of fold. Tug gently to form head of butterfly (*Diagram 3*). Both sides of body should have same size tuck, and center of body should be aligned with diagonal of block. Wings should angle away from head and tips should align with opposite diagonal of block (*Block Diagram*).

4. When satisfied with placement, pin in place. Appliqué to background. Satin-stitch head. Embroider antennae, using *Antennae Pattern*. Block should measure 16½".

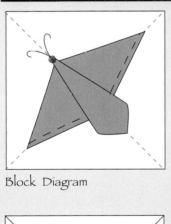

Block Diagram

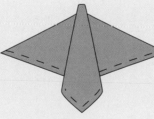

Diagram 3 (front)

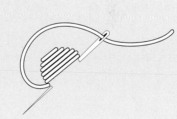

Satin-stitch Diagram

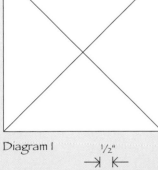

Diagram I

½"

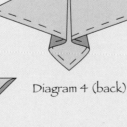

Diagram 4 (back)

Diagram 2
Back view of handkerchief

Antennae Pattern

Aunt Ginny's Handkerchief Quilt

This quilt belongs to Virginia Weaver of Dalton, Georgia. The focal point of the quilt is a handkerchief she's had since child-hood, and the buttons are from the collection of Louise F. Richards, her mother.

Aunt Ginny's Handkerchief Quilt

Finished Size: 25½" x 25½"

Materials
⅜ yard muslin for center and
   middle border
¾ yard purple print for borders
   and binding
32 (2½"-square) assorted prints
30" square fabric for backing
30" square batting

Cutting
Measurements include ¼" seam
allowances. Border strips are exact
length needed. You may want to
cut them longer to allow for piecing variations. Cut fabric selvage to
selvage unless otherwise noted.

From muslin, cut:
- 1 (12") square for center.
- 2 (1½" x 18") strips for middle
  side borders.
- 2 (1½" x 20") strips for middle
  top and bottom borders.

From purple print, cut:
- 2 (1½"-wide) strips. Cut strips
  into:
  - 2 (1½" x 12") strips for inner
    side borders.
  - 2 (1½" x 14") strips for inner
    top and bottom borders.
- 3 (3½"-wide) strips. Cut strips
  into:
  - 2 (3½" x 20") strips for outer
    side borders.
  - 2 (3½" x 26") strips for outer
    top and bottom borders.
- 3 (2¼"-wide) strips for binding.

Quilt Assembly
1. Appliqué handkerchief to 12"
muslin square.
2. Add 1½"-wide purple borders to
sides and then to top and bottom.
3. Join 7 (2½") squares into a row.

*When you appliqué embellishments to a memory quilt, match the thread as
closely as possible. This keeps the focus on the memorabilia, where it should be.*

Repeat. Add to quilt sides, trimming to fit.
4. Join 9 (2½") squares into a row.
Repeat. Add to top and bottom,
trimming to fit.
5. Add 1½"-wide muslin borders
to quilt sides and then to top and
bottom.
6. Repeat with 3½"-wide purple
borders.

Quilting and Finishing
1. Layer backing, batting, and quilt
top; baste.
2. Stitch vintage buttons through
all quilt layers. Add other embellishments as desired.
3. Quilt as desired. Quilt shown
was tacked in the middle with

buttons and outline-quilted around
patchwork and borders.
4. Join 2¼"-wide purple strips into
1 continuous piece for straight-
grain French-fold binding. Add
binding to quilt.

*Many women do
noble things, but
you surpass
them all.*

—*Proverbs 31:29*

T-Shirt Quilts

Almost all of us have them—a drawer full of old T-shirts that date back
to our college years or represent events we've attended. They have too much sentimental
value to part with, yet they take up valuable storage space.
If this sounds familiar, it's time to make a T-shirt quilt!

Directions for Making T-Shirt Quilts

Ideal Gifts

Even if T-shirt quilts aren't quite to your taste, you'll find that they make wonderful gifts. Think how much a high school or college graduate would appreciate a cuddly memento of his or her school days! Or you may have a nephew who participates in sports who would enjoy a quilt made from his jerseys. Perhaps a teen has T-shirts from rock concerts that would make a striking throw. A family member who camps could have shirts from various parks around the country. Maybe even your quilting buddy has shirts from major quilt shows that she's attended. Because each group of T-shirts represents a person's favorite places, groups, or events, you'll be making them a highly personalized memento that they will cherish for years.

Choosing Fabric

You have two options with a T-shirt quilt: you can either use T-shirts only on the quilt top, or you can sash it with 100% cotton fabric. Choosing fabrics in school colors for binding, backing, sashing, or block framing is a nice touch for a graduation quilt and an easy way to guarantee that the fabrics coordinate with the T-shirts.

One thing you will definitely need is a lot of lightweight fusible interfacing, available in sewing shops. Try to find a bolt that says it is for knits. If this is not available, any lightweight fusible interfacing will work. This material is not as wide as fabric, so you will need at least twice as much interfacing as you would fabric. If you are plan-ning a lap-size quilt, begin by pur-chasing 8 yards of interfacing. This material is not expensive, so buy as much as you can. Nothing is more frustrating than not being able to finish your project because you ran out of interfacing!

Instructions

1. Cut along side seams of shirt. Cut off sleeves and neck ribbing (Photo A). Discard neck ribbing and other pieces that don't contain images or writing.

Photo A

2. Cut a piece of lightweight fusible interfacing at least 2" larger than desired block size. (For example, for a 14"-square finished block, cut 16" or 17" square of interfacing.) This allows you leeway when cut-ting block from shirt.
3. Center interfacing on wrong side of shirt over design area. Following manufacturer's instructions, fuse interfacing to wrong side of T-shirt (Photo B).
4. Turn shirt over so right side of shirt faces you. Place a large rotary-cutting square over design area and center within frame of block size you intend to cut (Photo C).

Remember to add ½" for seam allowance.
5. Use rotary cutter to cut block to desired size (Photo D).

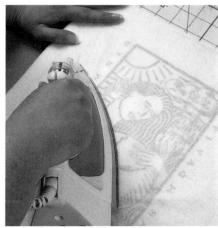

Photo B

Photo C

Photo D

Barry's Memory Quilt

Elsie Gilliland of Robertsdale, Alabama, made this quilt for her son, Barry Gilliland. "Barry's quilt takes his life memories from 1958 to 1992," says Elsie. "The quilt is machine-assembled and hand-quilted by me. It was a Christmas gift to Barry in 1996."

Barry's Memory Quilt

Finished Size: 65" x 89"

Elsie Gilliland's son Barry graduated from Auburn University, so she made the quilt in his school colors: blue and orange. She assembled the quilt in vertical rows and then joined the rows.

"Basically, it is a T-shirt quilt from events he took part in," says Elsie. "I included a picture of him at 16 months old on a train engine in Chapman, Alabama, as well as photos from high school, college graduation, and his wedding." See page 135 for photo transfer instructions.

Elsie appliquéd his school letters and patches and tacked on his pins from Little League.

Mothers of little boys

work from son up to son down.

—*Source unknown*

Not Your Run-of-the-Mill Quilt

Lauren Caswell Brooks, of Birmingham, Alabama, ran so many races that her drawers overflowed with commemorative race T-shirts. "I didn't want to throw any of them away, so I decided to preserve them by making a quilt," she says. She cut the T-shirt fronts into 14" squares and put 2"-wide black sashing strips between them to look like roads. To make this truly a runner's quilt, Lauren appliquéd running shoe shapes along the road.

College Memories

"I'm bad about holding on to things of sentimental value," says Rhonda Richards. "It struck me as a little pathetic, however, to realize that I was holding on to clothes with sentimental value! Even though they no longer fit and they're about 10 years old, I just couldn't bear to give up my college T-shirts and sorority jerseys.

"My solution was to turn them into a 'scrapbook quilt.' The most difficult part was planning the quilt, because the design areas were not uniform from shirt to shirt. So I tried to cut them in 6", 12", 14", and 16" blocks, plus some shorter strips that had my name (from the backs of jerseys).

"Even though the quilt pretty much worked out in the end, I still had to use a few spacers between blocks."

Roy Colley, of New Traditions machine quilting, "graffiti-quilted" this project. He quilted angels over Rhonda's sorority shirts, because that was her sorority's mascot, and dancing figures over her party shirts. Other touches include her name, graduation year, and Greek letters. He stippled some areas and left the pockets open.

Photo Transfer Quilts

You can make a scrapbook quilt easily with photo transfer paper and a color copier.
Following are instructions for making photo transfers yourself. Then use the quilts
featured in this section as inspiration in creating your own unique photo transfer quilt.

General Instructions for Photo Transfer

Preparing Your Photos

1. Arrange as many pictures as possible on a plain piece of paper (not the transfer paper), as shown in Photo A. Use a small piece of tape on the back of each photo to secure it to the paper.

Photo A

2. You must use a color copier—even if your photos are in black and white. Set the copier for mirror image. If the copier lacks this feature, you can make a transparency first and then print onto the transfer paper.
3. Make a test on plain copier paper to see which side of the photo transfer paper should be up.
4. Hand-feed the photo transfer paper into the machine. Make only 1 copy at a time. Copy onto the coated (unprinted) side of the transfer paper. You will have a mirror image (Photo B).

Photo B

Transferring to Fabric

1. Set your iron on the cotton setting. Do not use steam.
2. Cut apart your pictures on the photo transfer paper with scissors (Photo C) and then square them up with an old rotary cutter.

Photo C

3. Use the best and smoothest muslin you can find (200 thread count is best). Do not prewash the fabric. Cut a piece of muslin for each photo, leaving about 1" excess around all edges. You will trim this to size later.
4. Place the photo transfer facedown and press firmly with a hot iron for 30 seconds (Photo D). It is important to press hard to ensure a good image.

Photo D

5. While the paper is still hot, quickly peel off the paper, starting at one corner (Photo E). If after 30 seconds the paper will not come off, continue to press another 30 seconds and then peel the paper

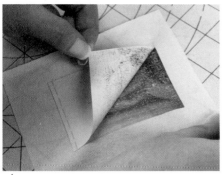

Photo E

off. Let the fabric cool briefly and press again, using medium heat and normal pressure.

Finishing

1. Rotary-cut ¼" seam allowances around all sides of photo transfer (Photo F).
2. Now play with your creativity to lay out a quilt.

Photo F

Other Ideas

Any noncopyrighted material that can be photocopied can be used for photo transfer: family recipe cards, newspaper clippings, children's art, documents, or letters. For example, if you are making an anniversary quilt, it might be a nice touch to add the marriage certificate or even some love letters.

Mother's Day Quilt

Rhonda Richards made this quilt as a Mother's Day surprise for her mother, Mona Richards. "I think my mother is so beautiful," says Rhonda, "and I wanted to show her just how glamorous she is. I had to sneak photos from her house and from my sister to make the quilt. I also made a point of using fabrics in colors that she likes."

Mother's Day Quilt

Materials

Photographs
1½ yards muslin
¼ to ⅜ yard each of 16 assorted fabrics for sashing
½ yard solid tan for inner border
1⅜ yards floral print for outer border
¾ yard hunter green for binding
4¾ yards fabric for backing
Batting

The blocks shown here (including the sashing around each photo) measure 12" x 15". With the borders, this made a 61" x 76" lap/twin quilt. If you use a different number or size of photos, you will need to do some simple planning to estimate how much fabric you will need for your own quilt.

General Instructions

Measurements include ¼" seam allowances. Border strips are exact length needed. You may want to cut them longer to allow for piecing variations. Cut fabric selvage to selvage unless otherwise noted.

1. Have copy center enlarge photo images as close to 8½" x 11" as possible. Have them transfer images to muslin (can be 1 large length or cut to 9" x 11½" pieces). (Or see page 135 for do-it-yourself instructions.)
2. Cut apart muslin images, cutting ¼" from image edge.
3. Cut assorted fabrics for sashing into 5"-wide strips. Join sashing strips to sides of photo first and then to top and bottom.
4. Trim all blocks to a uniform size (for example, 12½" x 15½"). By adding sashing strips first and then trimming blocks to size, all photos will be fairly centered in the

blocks, even though the photos themselves are different sizes.
5. Arrange blocks into rows as desired. Join blocks into horizontal rows. Then join rows. Quilt shown alternates green and gold framed blocks.
6. Cut tan fabric into 6 (2½"-wide) strips for inner border. Piece as necessary to make 2 (2½" x 60½") side borders and 2 (2½" x 52½") borders for top and bottom. Add borders to quilt sides and then to top and bottom.
7. Cut floral print into 7 (6½"-wide) strips for outer border. Piece as necessary to make 4 (6½" x 64½") borders. Add borders to quilt sides and then to top and bottom.

Quilting and Finishing

1. Divide backing fabric into 2 equal lengths. Cut 1 panel in half lengthwise. Join 1 narrow panel to each side of wide panel.
2. Layer backing, batting, and quilt top. Baste. Quilt as desired. Quilt shown has diagonal grid in sashing, except over photos. There is a small pattern in inner border and a cable in outer border.
3. Cut binding fabric into 8 (2¼"-wide) strips for binding. Piece into 1 continuous strip for straight-grain French-fold binding. Add binding to quilt.

Happy 50th Anniversary

Jody K. Schult of Overland Park, Kansas, made this quilt for her parents' (Leona and George McHargue, Sr.) 50th wedding anniversary. The photo transfer images include their wedding picture, high school graduations, family photos, and photos of their children. The appliquéd books represent their high school yearbooks, a family history book, and the Bible. "The two lace doilies are ones my mother made just after graduating high school," says Jody. "The gray 'sower' (the statue on the top left shelf) is the symbol of the insurance company that my father worked for." Turn to page 159 to see the label she designed. Finished Size: 49½" x 55".

Memories for Mother

Diane DeBolt of Palm Harbor, Florida, made this quilt as a Christmas present for her mother. In addition to using photo transfer techniques, Diane included embellishments such as buttons, silk ribbon embroidery, and crocheted pieces from her grandmother's sewing box. Finished Size: 45" x 48".

80th Birthday Quilt

Gloria Oliveira Denton of Modesto, California, combined traditional patchwork with modern photo transfer techniques to make this quilt for her mother-in-law, Nelia Mae Lazenby Denton. "I chose to reverse-appliqué the pictures to the blocks so they would look like pictures placed in an old album," says Gloria.

80th Birthday Quilt

Finished Size: 58" x 70"
Blocks: 31 (6") Nine-Patch and 32 (6") Snowball Blocks

Materials

2½ yards white-on-white for background and borders (3½ yards for unpieced borders)
¾ yard pink print
1 yard blue print
2 yards navy print (3½ yards for unpieced borders)
4½ yards fabric for backing
Twin-size batting
28 photos, transferred to fabric

Nine-Patch Block Diagram

Cutting

Measurements include ¼" seam allowances. Border strips are exact length needed. Cut fabric selvage to selvage unless otherwise noted.

From white on white, cut:
- 8 (2½"-wide) strips. Cut strips into 124 (2½") squares for Nine-Patch blocks.
- 6 (6½"-wide) strips. Cut strip into 32 (6½") squares for Snowball blocks.
- 2 (3¼"-wide) strips. Cut strips into 14 (3¼") squares. Cut squares in quarters diagonally to make 56 quarter-square triangles for pieced border. You will have 2 extra.
- 5 (2½"-wide) strips for border. Piece as needed to make 2 (2½" x 54½") side borders and 2 (2½" x 46½") top and bottom

Gloria Oliveira Denton used pictures from her mother-in-law's childhood through her adulthood, including her children, grandchildren, and great-grandchildren, whose names appear at the bottom of the quilt.

borders. If you prefer unpieced borders, cut 1⅝ yards from alternate yardage, and cut 4 (2½"-wide) lengthwise strips.

From pink print, cut:
- 1 (6"-wide) strip. Cut strip into 4 (6") squares for heart appliqués.
- 2 (2⅞"-wide) strips. Cut strips into 25 (2⅞") squares. Cut squares in half diagonally to make 50 half-square triangles for pieced border.
- 2 (3¼"-wide) strips. Cut strips into 14 (3¼") squares. Cut

squares in quarters diagonally to make 56 quarter-square triangles for pieced border. You will have 2 extra.

From blue print, cut:
- 8 (2½"-wide) strips. Cut strips into 128 (2½") squares for Snowball corners.
- 2 (2⅞"-wide) strips. Cut strips into 28 (2⅞") squares. Cut squares in half diagonally to make 56 half-square triangles for pieced border.
- 1 (3¼"-wide) strip. Cut strip

into 12 (3¼") squares. Cut squares in quarters diagonally to make 48 quarter-square triangles for pieced border.

From navy print, cut:

- 6 (4½"-wide) strips for border. Piece to make 2 (4½" x 62½") side borders and 2 (4½" x 58½") top and bottom borders. If you prefer unpieced borders, cut 2 yards from alternate yardage. Cut 4 (4½"-wide) lengthwise strips and proceed.
- 10 (2½"-wide) strips. Cut strips into 155 (2½") squares for Nine-Patch blocks.
- 1 (3¼"-wide) strip. Cut strip into 12 (3¼") squares. Cut squares in quarters diagonally to make 48 quarter-square triangles for pieced border.
- 2 (2⅞") squares. Cut squares in half diagonally to make 4 half-square triangles for pieced border corners.
- 7 (2¼"-wide) strips for binding.

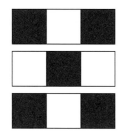

Nine-Patch Block
Assembly Diagram

Block Assembly

Nine-Patch Blocks

1. Lay out 5 navy print squares and 4 white-on-white squares as shown in *Nine-Patch Block Assembly Diagram*. Join into rows; join rows to make 1 Nine-Patch block.
2. Make 31 Nine-Patch blocks.

Snowball Block
Diagram

Snowball Block Assembly Diagrams

Snowball Blocks

1. Using diagonal seams method and referring to *Snowball Block Assembly Diagrams*, align 1 blue print square on 1 corner of 1 (6½") white-on-white square. Stitch across diagonal, trim, and open out. Repeat on all 4 corners.
2. Make 32 Snowball blocks (*Snowball Block Diagram*).
3. Reverse-appliqué (or regular appliqué) photos and hearts to centers of each block. To reverse appliqué, place photo under white center of block. Decide what shape best frames the photo (such as an oval or circle) and carefully mark just

inside area with a pencil. Leave ¼" inside for seam allowance, and cut away center section. Turn edge to the back and appliqué to photo transfer fabric, clipping as needed.

Make 24.   Make 24.   Make 2.

Make 27.   Make 27.   Make 2.

Border Block Diagrams

Border Assembly

Refer to *Border Block Diagrams* throughout.

1. Join 1 navy quarter-square triangle to 1 blue print quarter-square triangle to make a half-square triangle. Make 24 with navy on right and 24 with navy on left. Join each unit with a pink half-square triangle to make 48 pink/navy/blue border units.
2. Join 1 white quarter-square

Quilt Top Assembly Diagram

triangle to 1 pink quarter-square triangle to make a half-square triangle. Make 27 with white on right and 27 with white on left. Join each unit to 1 blue print half-square triangle to make 54 blue/white/pink border units.

3. Join 1 pink and 1 navy half-square triangle to make 1 corner unit. Make 2 pink/navy corner units.

4. Join 1 blue and 1 navy half-square triangle to make 1 corner unit. Make 2 blue/navy corner units.

5. Carefully refer to borders in *Quilt Top Assembly Diagram* to assemble 4 borders, placing blocks as shown. Use a scant ¼" seam allowance when assembling top and bottom borders.

Quilt Assembly

1. Alternate Nine-Patch blocks and Snowball blocks as shown in *Quilt Top Assembly Diagram*. Arrange photos as desired. Place heart Snowball blocks in each corner. Join into rows; join rows to complete center.

2. Add white-on-white side borders. Add white-on-white top and bottom borders.

3. Add side pieced borders. Add top and bottom pieced borders.

4. Add navy side borders. Add navy top and bottom borders.

Quilting and Finishing

1. Divide backing fabric into 2 (2¼ - yard) lengths. Cut 1 piece in half lengthwise. Sew 1 narrow panel to 1 side of wide panel. Press seam allowances toward narrow panel. Remaining panel is extra.

2. Layer backing, batting, and quilt top; baste. Quilt as desired. Quilt shown was quilted in-the-ditch and has a heart pattern in border.

3. Join 2¼"-wide navy strips into 1 continuous piece for straight-grain French-fold binding. Add binding to quilt.

80th Birthday Quilt
BLOCK BY BLOCK

Instructions for 1 (6") Nine-Patch Block and 1 (6") Snowball Block

Nine-Patch Block Diagram

Nine-Patch Block Assembly Diagram

Snowball Block Diagram

Snowball Block Assembly Diagrams

MATERIALS
1 fat eighth* each white-on-white, blue print, navy print
Photo transferred to fabric or 1 (6") square pink print for heart
*Fat eighth = 9" x 22"

CUTTING
From white-on-white, cut:
• 4 (2½") squares for Nine-Patch.
• 1 (6½") square for Snowball.
From blue print, cut:
• 4 (2½") squares for Snowball.
From navy, cut:
• 5 (2½") squares for Nine-Patch.

NINE-PATCH BLOCK ASSEMBLY
Lay out 5 navy print squares and 4 white-on-white squares as shown in *Nine-Patch Block Assembly Diagram*. Join into rows; join rows to make 1 Nine-Patch block. Block should measure 6½".

SNOWBALL BLOCK ASSEMBLY
1. Using diagonal seams method, align 1 blue print square on 1 corner of 1 (6½") white-on-white square. Stitch across diagonal, trim, and open out. Repeat on 4 corners.

2. Reverse-appliqué photo/heart to center of block. To reverse appliqué, place photo under white center of block. Decide what shape best frames the photo (such as an oval or circle) and carefully mark just inside area with a pencil. Leave ¼" inside for seam allowance and cut away center section. Turn edge to the back and appliqué to photo transfer fabric, clipping as needed. Block should measure 6½".

Fond Memories

Helen Blakeley, of Scarborough, Ontario, began Fond Memories *as a signature quilt for students who attended St. Marys Collegiate Institute in St. Marys, Ontario, Canada. Helen took the top to their 1997 high school reunion for her former classmates to sign. After the 2000 reunion, Helen will donate the quilt to St. Marys Museum. At the reunion several alumni brought old photos and newspaper articles from their school days. Helen borrowed the memorabilia and had them transferred onto fabric. Using these, she created yet another school quilt. She and her sister Leota Hicks quilted each of the quilts separately, joined them back to back, and then bound them.*

Fond Memories

Finished Size:
61" x 67¾"
(See page 40 for quilt's reverse side that features signature blocks.)

Helen used her computer to print out the quilt label (see page 150). She made the label into a buttoned pocket. Inside is a list of all her classmates and information about the school.

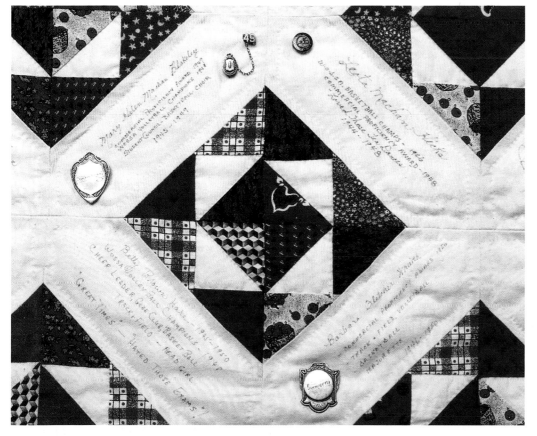

Helen added memorabilia to her quilt, such as old school pins and recognition pieces. She included information about each piece on the block to which it was attached.

In the Sewing Room

Having the right tools will increase your enjoyment of quilting and improve your accuracy. New products are constantly appearing on the market, but below is a list of must-haves to get you started.

CUTTING TOOLS

Rotary Cutter: Purchase a cutter with at least a 2"-diameter blade. The larger cutters allow you to cut through more layers. Look at the instructions on the back of the package to see the proper way to hold the brand you bought.

Cutting Mat: Purchase the largest mat you can afford. Make sure you at least have one that measures 18" x 24".

Cutting Rulers: The longer you quilt, the more of these you will buy. Start with a 6" x 24" ruler. Later you may want to add a 6" square, a 12½" square, and a triangle ruler.

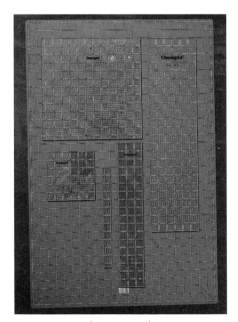

Large mat and various rulers

Cutting Table: Make your work-table a comfortable height for standing while you cut and work. Most people like a cutting table about 36" high. Some tables are available with collapsible sides to conserve space when not in use.

Thread Clippers: Trim threads quickly with this spring-action tool.

Fabric Shears: A fine pair of sharp fabric shears will become one of your treasured possessions. To keep them sharp, do not cut anything but fabric with them.

Paper Scissors: Use an inexpensive pair of large, sharp scissors to cut paper, template plastic, and cardboard—everything except fabric.

Appliqué Scissors: The duckbill piece at the bottom helps you to trim background fabrics away from appliqué shapes.

Shown from left to right: thread clippers, fabric shears, paper scissors, and appliqué scissors

SEWING TOOLS

Sewing Machine: Unless you plan to do machine appliqué, a good straight-stitch sewing machine is all you'll need.

Needles: Replace the needle in your sewing machine regularly. Size 80/12 is just right for machine piecing. For handwork, use a size 10 or 11 **sharp** for hand appliqué and a 10 or 12 **between** for hand quilting.

Walking foot

Walking Foot: If you plan to machine-quilt, you must have a walking foot to feed the quilt layers through your machine evenly.

Thread: Use cotton thread for piecing and quilting. You'll find that neutral colors—white, beige, or gray—work with most quilts.

Pins: Spend a few extra dollars to get fine silk pins. These pins are so thin, you can usually keep them in your fabric and sew over them with most sewing machines.

Portable steam iron

PRESSING TOOLS

Iron: Look for a steam iron that produces plenty of steam.

Plastic Squirt Bottle: Some fabrics need a spray of water in addition to the steam from the iron.

Ironing Board: An ironing board or large pressing pad at one end of your cutting table will enable you to stand and to press at a comfortable height.

Organizing a Signature Quilt & Making Templates

ORGANIZING A SIGNATURE QUILT

If you will be making all the blocks yourself, stabilize the signature pieces (see page 149) and distribute them to your friends. If a group of quilters will be making the blocks, refer to the "Block by Block" instructions for the pattern you chose.

- If the quilt will have a uniform background (as opposed to scrappy), buy more of that fabric than you need. That way, you can cut more pieces if some get lost or soiled.
- Purchase several Pigma™ pens. We recommend using the .05 width. The tip is wider than the .01 size, making the writing more visible and less likely to fade in the wash.
- Decide how many blocks you need and make a list of all participants.
- Mark people off your list as they return their signature piece or quilt block so that you'll know who to follow up with.
- If quilters are making blocks for you, be sure to set a theme for the quilt, whether by color or fabric type. If you simply ask them to use their favorite fabrics, you'll end up with neons, reproduction prints, and novelty prints, and the quilt will lack cohesiveness.
- If the quilt will be a gift, try to use colors to suit that person's taste, not yours.

ADAPTING THE QUILT SIZE

If the quilt you plan to make is not the size you want, there are several ways to adapt the design.

To make a smaller quilt, eliminate a row of blocks, set the blocks without sashing, and/or narrow the border widths.

To make a larger quilt, add rows of blocks, sashing, and/or multiple borders. Each addition requires extra yardage, which you should estimate before you buy fabric. Since most of the quilts in this book have "Block by Block" instructions, it should be easy to calculate how much more fabric you need.

HOW TO USE OUR PATTERNS

Oxmoor House patterns are full size. Patterns for pieced blocks show the seam line (dashed) and the cutting line (solid). Appliqué patterns do not include seam allowances.

MAKING TEMPLATES

Almost all of the quilts in this book can be made with rotary-cutting instructions. However, a few do require templates. You can make templates from traditional template plastic or from cardboard.

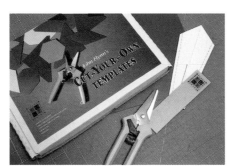

Cut-Your Own Templates Kit

However, we have found a new product that allows you to make your own templates and still use a rotary cutter to cut the fabric! Designed by John Flynn, Cut-Your-Own Templates™ are made of formica (see Resources on page 160). The kit includes several sheets of formica and everything you need to make any template shape. The formica is thick enough that you can use your rotary cutter to cut along its edge. This set is ideal for making quilts like *Friendship Star* on page 44.

APPLIQUÉ

Appliqué is the process of sewing pieces onto a background to create a fabric picture.

Use the drawn line as a guide.

Slipstitch around each piece.

HAND APPLIQUÉ

For traditional hand appliqué, use the drawn line as a guide to turn under seam allowances on each piece. Do not turn an edge that will be covered by another piece. Hand-baste the seam allowances. You can eliminate basting, if you prefer, and rely on rolling the edge under with the tip of your needle as you sew. This is called needle-turned appliqué. Pin appliqué pieces to the background.

Slipstitch around each piece, using thread that matches the

appliqué. (We used contrasting thread for photography.) Pull the needle through the background and catch a few threads on the fold of the appliqué. Reinsert the needle into the background and bring the needle up through the appliqué for the next stitch. Make close, tiny stitches that do not show on the right side. Remove basting.

FREEZER-PAPER APPLIQUÉ

In using this technique, the finished appliqué will be a mirror image of the pattern. So, if the pattern is an irregular shape (not symmetrical), first reverse the pattern. Trace a full-size pattern onto the paper (nonwaxy) side of freezer paper. Cut out each freezer-paper template along the drawn lines.

When you press the seam allowances over the freezer paper, we recommend using a product called GluTube®. If you've ever used a glue stick with freezer paper to temporarily "baste" the seam allowances, you'll discover that GluTube® works much the same way. However, it is not gooey once it dries, and it will not stick to your fingers and make a mess like a glue stick can. It also allows you to create sharp, smooth edges on your appliqué. Here's how it works:

1. Press the freezer-paper template to the wrong side of the appliqué fabric.

Step 1

2. Apply GluTube® in a circular motion, covering approximately ¼" of the edges along both the template and the fabric. Let the glue dry for a few minutes.

Step 2

3. Cut out the template, adding ¼" seam allowance. Don't worry about cutting into the glue—once dry, it has the same consistency as the adhesive on yellow sticky notes.

Step 3

4. Clip curves or points as needed. Using a straight pin, fold the seam allowances over the edge of the template. Use your fingers to gently set the temporary bond. You may lift and reposition the fabric as needed.

Step 4

5. Appliqué the shape to the background as usual. Clip the background fabric from behind the appliquéd shape and gently remove the freezer paper with tweezers. The template will release easily.

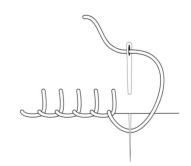

Step 5

GluTube® is available in quilt shops and through The Quilt Farm (see Resources, page 160).

FUSIBLE APPLIQUÉ

If you do not enjoy handwork, fusing appliqué shapes with paper-backed fusible web may be an option for you. Follow manufacturer's instructions on the package. You will still need to cover the fabric edges so that they will not ravel when the quilt is washed. You can do this with a machine satin stitch or with a hand or machine blanket-stitch.

Blanket Stitch Diagram

Signing Blocks & Using Rubber Stamps

SIGNING BLOCKS

To sign blocks, you will need freezer paper (available in grocery stores near the aluminum foil) and colorfast, fabric-safe pens (see Resources on page 160).

1. To stabilize the fabric for writing, press a piece of freezer paper to the back.

2. Use a thick-pointed permanent pen to draw a line on the paper side of the freezer paper to give you a writing guideline that will be visible through the fabric.

3. Using a colorfast, fabric-safe pen (like Pigma™), write lightly and slowly to allow the ink to flow and to prevent the pen from catching in the weave of the cloth (fabric is rougher than paper). Let the ink dry.

4. Heat-set the ink with a hot, dry iron on the back of the fabric.

Use rubber stamps for creative labels.

USING RUBBER STAMPS

Stamping is a fun and easy way to add decoration and documentation to your quilts. In adapting stamping to our quilts, we are joining a historic tradition of quilt decoration. Quilters of the mid-nineteenth century used stamps to embellish their signature quilts.

To successfully stamp on fabric, the stamp design must be deeply etched into the rubber. Many stamps designed for paper stamping are not deeply etched. As a result, the image may be pale and the details lost on fabric. Stamps made by Susan McKelvey (see Resources, page 160) meet these requirements, and several of her stamps were used on quilts in this book.

Make sure that the ink you use is colorfast and fabric-safe. We recommend Fabrico™ ink, which is available in 12 colors on preinked stamp pads (see Resources, page 160).

STAMPING BLOCKS

Practice on a fabric scrap to see how much ink you need and how much pressure to apply. Stamp on a hard, flat surface.

1. When inking the stamp, hold the stamp up and the stamp pad down as shown in Photo A. This enables you to control how much ink you put on the stamp.

2. Tap the pad gently against the stamp. Press lightly several times,

Photo A: Hold the stamp under the pad while inking.

rather than hard once, to prevent applying excess ink.

3. Stamp the fabric by pressing firmly; don't rock the stamp.

4. Let the ink dry. It dries quickly to the touch (Photo B).

Photo B: The finished results look professional.

5. Heat-set the ink with a hot, dry iron on the back of the fabric.

USING COMPUTERS

If you own a home computer, try using it to print designs on your blocks and quilt labels. If you don't like your handwriting, or if you just want to add some creative lettering, your computer will have a wide range of fonts to choose from. Below is a quick review of terms to help get you started. Most of these items will be under the "Style" menu at the top of your computer screen. Because brands differ, these are only general descriptions to get you started. You will need to use your computer manual or consult your computer dealer if you need specific information.

USEFUL THINGS TO KNOW

A **font** is the print style you use for the letters. Most word processing programs will come with a wide variety of fonts. Regardless of the font you choose, you can make it bold or italic, if desired.

The **size** determines how large your fonts will be. Normally, you don't want to use a size smaller than 10 or 12 points (pt) for the text to be read easily. Experiment to see how large you can go. For a quilt label, you might consider putting the quilt's name in 36 pt; your name, date, and residence in 24 pt; and the text describing the quilt in 12 pt. (See the label above.)

Depending on whether or not you have a **color printer,** you can print items in color. However, run a test to see if your printer has color-fast ink. Most do not, although most black inks tend to be colorfast. Check with your computer dealer to see if colorfast ink is available for your printer.

Never use noncolorfast ink in a

quilt block. However, if you choose to use it for a quilt label, be sure to print yourself a small note in red at the bottom of the label reminding you to remove it before laundering. A better option is to print the design in colorfast black and then color in with Pigma™ pens.

Most computers also come with **clipart.** If not, the software is widely available (and inexpensive) at office supply and computer stores.

You may also obtain images and fonts from the **Internet.** Download the images onto your computer. Watch for charges, though. There are many items you can download free, so only pay for fonts you really love. Don't be afraid of the Internet. Unless you are asked to enter a credit card number, you will not be charged for the fonts. Some sites allow you to download fonts free for 30 days. At the end of that time, they simply disappear from your computer.

If you own a **scanner,** your possibilities are nearly endless. Any image you can scan can be transferred to fabric.

PRINTING ON FABRIC

You can print what's on your screen directly onto your fabric. You are not limited to muslin; you can use any 100% cotton fabric, as long as it is light enough for the ink to show. *Note: Oxmoor House does not assume any responsibility for damage caused to your printer trying these techniques. If your printer jams on paper, do not try to feed it fabric. Do not use these techniques at work with equipment that is not your own.*

The quilt labels shown in this book were made on a Windows 95 compatible home PC, using an HP Inkjet 820 color printer. The text came from Microsoft Works™ for Windows 95, and the clipart is Microsoft ClipArt Gallery 2.0.

1. Design a quilt label on your screen. Enter text in your favorite font, varying the size as desired.
2. Under your menu bar, find "Insert" and scroll down to "Clipart." Select the desired image, and click on "OK" or "Insert"

Using Computers

Photo A

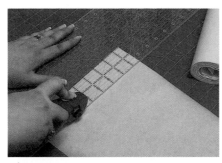

Photo C

Photo F

Photo B

Photo D

Photo G

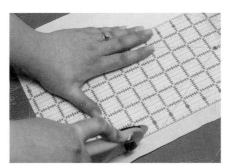

Photo E

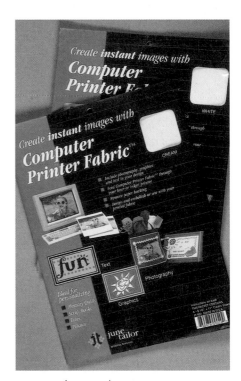

New products make printing computer images to fabric fast and easy.

(Photo A). The image should now be in your quilt label text (Photo B).

3. Adjust text and image sizes as needed. Print a sample on paper to see if you're happy with it. Experiment to determine if your paper feeds into the printer face-up or facedown.

4. Using an old rotary cutter, cut a piece of freezer paper 8½" x 11" (Photo C). Using a hot, dry iron, press freezer paper to the wrong side of the fabric (Photo D).

5. Using your good rotary cutter, trim the fabric to 8½" x 11" (Photo E). Press outside edges again, to make sure the freezer paper is still secure. Check for extraneous threads along the edges and clip them, if needed.

6. Place the fabric sheet on top of the paper in your printer (Photo F).

7. Click on "Print." Your fabric should feed through the printer as paper would (Photo G).

8. Let the ink dry. Remove the freezer paper and then heat-set the ink with a hot, dry iron. Trim the image to size, if necessary.

There is a new product available called Computer Printer Fabric™ that feeds directly into your printer. Check local quilting and computer shops or order it from Connecting Threads (see Resources, page 160). It is available in white and cream.

Joining Blocks and Borders

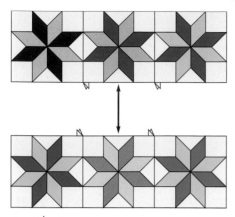

Straight Set

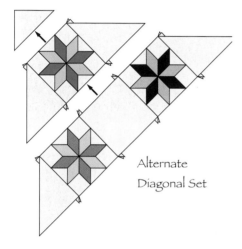

Alternate
Diagonal Set

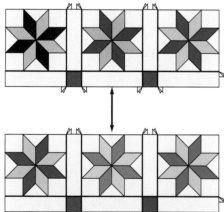

Sashed Blocks

JOINING BLOCKS

Arrange blocks and setting pieces on the floor, on a large table, or on a design wall. Identify the pieces in each row and verify the position of each block. This is the fun part—move the blocks around to find the best balance of color and value. Don't begin sewing until you're happy with the placement of each block.

1. Press seam allowances between blocks in a straight set in the same direction. From row to row, press in opposite directions so that seam allowances will offset when you join rows.

2. In an alternate set, straight or diagonal, press seam allowances between blocks toward setting squares or triangles. This creates the least bulk and always results in opposing seam allowances when you join adjacent rows.

3. Sashing eliminates questions about pressing. Just remember to always press toward the sashing. Assemble rows with sashing strips between blocks, pressing each new seam allowance toward the sashing. If necessary, ease the block to match the strip. Assemble the quilt with sashing rows between block rows.

BORDERS

Most quilts have borders, which help frame the quilt. They can be plain, pieced, or appliquéd, with square or mitered corners.

MEASURING

It's common for one side of a quilt top to be slightly different from the measurement on the opposite side. Even small discrepancies in cutting and piecing add up across the quilt. Sewing borders of equal length to opposite sides will square up the quilt.

When you cut lengthwise strips for borders, you'll want to measure your quilt before trimming the strips to the size indicated in the instructions. When you measure,

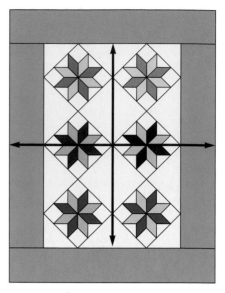

Measuring for Square Corners

measure down the center of the quilt rather than along the edges.

SQUARE CORNERS

Measure from top to bottom through the middle of the quilt as shown above. Trim side borders to this length and add them to the quilt sides. You may need to ease one side of a quilt to fit the border and stretch the opposite side to fit the same border length. In the end, both sides will be the same. Unless you're using a walking foot, your sewing machine naturally feeds the bottom layer through the feed dogs faster than it does the top layer. So always put the longer side (the side that needs to be eased in) on the bottom as you sew.

For top and bottom borders, measure from side to side through the middle of the quilt, including the side borders you just added and their seam allowance. Trim remaining border to this measurement and add them to the quilt.

Mitered Corners

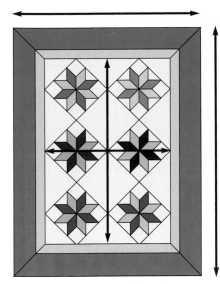

Measuring for Mitered Borders

Press the mitered corner seam flat.

MITERED CORNERS

The seam of a mitered corner is more subtle than that of a square corner, so it creates the illusion of a continuous line around the quilt. Mitered corners are ideal for striped borders, pieced borders, or multiple plain borders. Sew multiple borders together first and treat the resulting striped unit as a single border for mitering.

Sewing a Mitered Corner

1. Measure your quilt as described above. Add to this measurement the width of the border plus 2".
2. Place a pin on the center of the quilt side and another pin on the center of the border.
3. With right sides facing and raw edges aligned, match the pins on the border to the quilt. Working from the center out, pin border to quilt. The border will extend beyond the quilt edges. Do not trim it.
4. Sew border to quilt, backstitching at each end. Press seam allowance toward border. Join remaining borders in the same manner.
5. With right sides facing, fold the quilt diagonally as shown in *Mitering Diagram 1,* aligning the raw edges of adjacent borders. Pin securely.
6. Align a ruler along the diagonal fold as shown in *Mitering Diagram 2.* Holding the ruler firmly, mark a line from the end of the border seam to the raw edge.
7. Start machine-stitching at the beginning of the marked line, backstitch, and then stitch on the line out to the raw edge.
8. Unfold the quilt to be sure that the corner lies flat. Correct the stitching if necessary. Trim the seam allowance to ¼".
9. Miter the remaining corners. Press the corner seams flat.

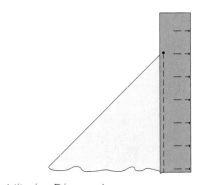

Mitering Diagram 1

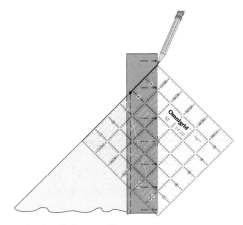

Mitering Diagram 2

PREPARING FOR QUILTING

The quilting design is an important part of any quilt, so choose it with care. The hours you spend stitching together the layers of your quilt create shadows and depths that bring the quilt to life, so make the design count.

In our "Quilting and Finishing" instructions, we tell you to "quilt as desired," but then we also tell you how the project shown was quilted. Since most of the intricate quilting designs were used from purchased stencils, we cannot reproduce the pattern within the book.

QUILTING WITHOUT MARKING

There are several ways to quilt that do not require you to mark the quilt top:

- **In-the-ditch:** Quilting right in the seam.
- **Outline Quilting:** Quilting ¼" from the seam line. You can "eyeball" this measurement or use ¼"-wide masking tape as a guide.
- **Grid Quilting:** Quilting in straight, diagonal lines, usually 1" apart. Using the 45° line on your ruler to get you started, place 1"-wide masking tape on your quilt and quilt along its edge. Never keep the tape on your quilt for long periods of time—if you must set your project aside for a time, remove the tape.
- **Stippling:** Freestyle, meandering lines of quilting worked closely together to fill open areas.

USING STENCILS

To find a stencil for a quilting design, check your local quilt shop

Using a stencil to mark a quilt design

or mail-order catalogs (see Resources, page 160) for one that suits your quilt.

To transfer a design to the quilt top, position the stencil on the quilt and mark through the slits in the stencil. Connect the lines after removing the stencil.

Before using any marker, test it on scraps to be sure marks will wash out. Don't use just any pencil.

There are many pencils and chalk markers available that are designed to wash out.

BATTING

Precut batting comes in five sizes. The precut batting listed for each quilt is the most suitable for the quilt's finished size. Some stores sell 90" batting by the yard, which might be more practical for your quilt.

Loft is the height or thickness of the batting. For a traditional, flat look, choose low-loft cotton batting. Thick batting is difficult to quilt, unless you plan to machine-quilt or tie it as a comforter.

Cotton batting provides the flat, thin look of an antique quilt, making it ideal for memory quilts.

Layering a quilt

Backing & Basting

Thread basting

Cotton shrinks slightly when washed, giving it that wrinkled look characteristic of all quilts.

Polyester batting is easy to stitch and can be washed with little shrinkage. However, look for the word "bonded" when selecting polyester batts. Bonding keeps the loft of the batt uniform and reduces the effects of bearding (migration of loose fibers through the quilt top). Avoid bonded batts that feel stiff.

BACKING

The instructions in this book tell you how to cut and piece standard 42"-wide fabric to make backing. The backing should be at least 3" larger than the top on all sides.

For a large quilt, 90"- or 108"-wide fabric is a sensible option that reduces waste and eliminates backing seams. Quilters are no longer limited to muslin; new wide fabrics are available in lovely prints.

Some quilters treat the backing as another design element of their quilt, choosing to piece interesting designs or appliqué large shapes.

LAYERING

Lay the backing right side down on a large work surface—a large table, two tables pushed together, or a clean floor. Use masking tape to secure the edges, keeping the backing wrinkle-free and slightly taut.

Smooth the batting over the backing; then trim the batting even with the backing. Center the pressed quilt top right side up on the batting. Make sure the edges of the backing and quilt top are parallel.

BASTING

Basting keeps layers from shifting during quilting. Baste with a long needle and white thread (colored thread can leave a residue on light fabrics). Or use safety pins, if you prefer.

Start in the center and baste a line of stitches to each corner, making a large X. Then baste parallel lines 6" to 8" apart. Finish with a line of basting ¼" from the edge.

Some quilters use nickel-plated safety pins for basting. Pin every 2" to 3". Don't close the pins as you go, as this can pucker the backing. When all pins are in place, remove the tape at the quilt edges. Gently tug the backing as you close each pin so that pleats don't form underneath.

Another popular method is to use a basting gun, which shoots plastic tabs through quilt layers. Use paper-cutting scissors to trim the tabs away after quilting is done.

Pin basting

Basting gun

Hand & Machine Quilting

QUILTING

Quilting is the process of stitching the layers of a quilt together, by hand or by machine. The choice of hand or machine quilting depends on the design of the quilt, how much time you have, and the quilt's intended use. The techniques differ, but the results of both are functional and attractive.

HAND QUILTING

To make a stitch, first insert the needle straight down (Photo A). With your other hand under the quilt, feel for the needle point as it pierces the backing. With practice, you'll be able to find the point without pricking your finger.

Roll the needle to a nearly horizontal position (Photo B). Use the thumb of your sewing hand and the underneath hand to pinch a little hill in the fabric as you push the needle back through the quilt top. Gently tug the thread to pop the knot into the quilt. Then rock the needle back to an upright position for the next stitch. Load 3 to 4 stitches on the needle before pulling it through.

With 6" of thread left, tie a knot close to the quilt top. Backstitch; then pop the knot into the batting. Run the thread through the batting and out the top to clip it.

MACHINE QUILTING

If you plan to machine quilt, you must have a walking foot for your sewing machine (Photo C). This allows all the quilt layers to feed through your machine evenly. Use this foot for straight-line quilting.

For free-motion quilting or stippling, you will need a darning foot (Photo D). Lower the feed dogs or cover them. You control the stitch length by manually moving the fabric.

Another option is to have someone who owns a professional quilting machine to quilt your project. Check your quilt shop or guild for local sources.

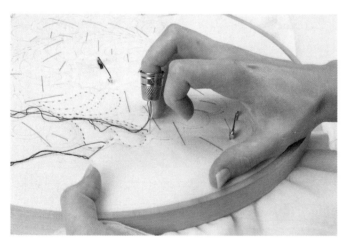

Photo A

Photo C

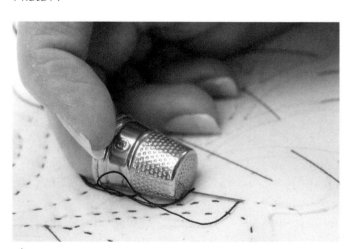

Photo B

Photo D

Binding

BINDING

There is a common misconception among quilters that quilts must have bias binding. This is not true. The only time a quilt must have bias binding is when it has curved edges or rounded corners. If you use a plaid for the binding and want the plaid to appear "on point," use bias binding.

All of the quilts in this book have straight edges, so straight-grain French-fold (or double-folded) binding is appropriate for all of them. This method uses less fabric and can even help your quilt hang straighter.

MAKING STRAIGHT-GRAIN BINDING

1. Cut needed number of strips selvage to selvage. Cut strips 2¼" wide when working with thin batting and 2½" wide when working with thicker fabric (like flannel) or batting.
2. Join strips end-to-end to make a continuous strip. To join 2 strips, layer them perpendicular to each other with right sides facing. Stitch a diagonal seam across strips as shown in *Diagram A*. Trim seam allowances to ¼" and press open.
3. Fold binding in half lengthwise with wrong sides facing. Press.

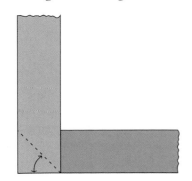

Diagram A

ADDING BINDING

Sew binding to the front of the quilt first by machine. Begin stitching in the middle of any quilt side. Do not trim excess batting and backing until after you stitch the binding on the quilt.
1. Matching raw edges, lay binding on quilt. Stitch binding to quilt, using ⅜" seam and leaving about 2" unstitched at the top *(Diagram B)*.

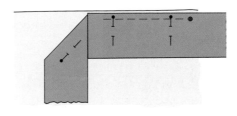

Diagram B

2. Continue stitching down side of quilt. Stop ⅜" from corner and backstitch. Remove quilt from machine and clip threads.
3. Fold binding strip straight up, away from quilt, making a 45° angle *(Diagram C)*.

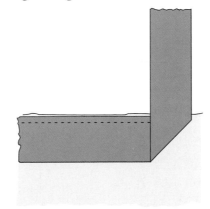

Diagram C

4. Fold binding straight down along next side to be stitched, creating fold that is even with raw edge of previously stitched side.
5. Begin stitching at top edge of new side *(Diagram D)*. Stitch length of new side. Continue until all 4 corners and sides are joined in this manner. Stop stitching ¼" from point where binding began. Trim excess binding, leaving a 2" tail. Join the 2 tails with diagonal seams *(Diagram E)*. Trim excess binding beyond diagonal stitching and press open. Stitch a straight line (as normal) over this area to secure the ¼" open space *(Diagram F)*.

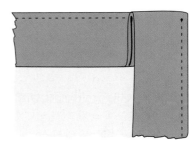

Diagram D

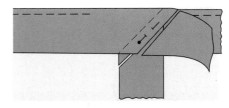

Diagram E

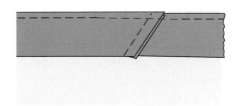

Diagram F

6. Trim excess batting and backing even with binding raw edge.
7. Turn binding over raw edge of quilt and slipstitch in place on backing with matching thread. At each corner, fold binding to form a miter. Whipstitch miter closed. (The miter should form naturally when you turn the corners to the back of the quilt.)

Bias Binding

MAKING BIAS BINDING

Step 1

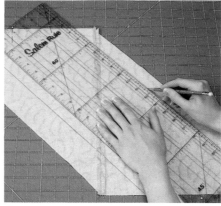

Step 3

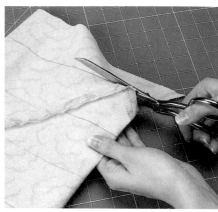

Step 5

1. To cut bias binding, start with a square. (For a queen-size quilt, a 32" square is sufficient.) Center pins at top and bottom edges with heads toward inside. At each side, center a pin with head toward outside edge. Cut square in half diagonally to make 2 triangles.

3. On wrong side of fabric, mark cutting lines parallel to long edges. Space between lines would equal the width of the desired strip (for example, 2¼").

5. Begin cutting at extended edge. Follow drawn lines, rolling tube around as you cut, until all fabric is cut into a continuous strip. See instructions on page 157 for adding binding to quilt.

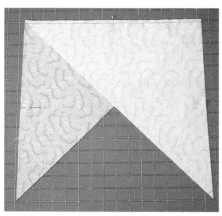

Step 2

Step 4

2. With right sides facing, match edges with pin heads pointed to outside. Remove pins and join triangles with a ¼" seam. Press seam open.

4. Match edges with pin heads pointed to inside, right sides facing, offsetting 1 width of binding strip as shown. Join edges with a ¼" seam to make a tube. Press seam open.

QUILT LABELS

It is unfortunate to come across any quilt, especially a signature quilt, in an antique shop with no record of the quilt's history. Every quilt you make should include a quilt label. You can appliqué or piece the label to the back, or include the information in a quilt block on the front.

At a minimum, your quilt label should include:

• the name of the quilt
• your name
• your city and state
• the date of completion, or the date of presentation

Additional information can include the story behind the quilt, the maker, and/or the recipient. Consider recording how old you were when you made the quilt.

There are numerous ways to embellish your quilt label. Look for ideas within this book, or use your computer (see page 150) to find images. Rubber stamps can be fun to use, too (see page 149).

You can add more labels if the quilt is displayed, published, or acknowledged with an award.

Even if you purchase an antique quilt, make a label. Research the pattern to see if you can determine the approximate date the quilt was made, or simply put "unknown." But at least put your name and the date and the place you purchased it for future reference.

Barbara Butler used photo transfer to make this label for the Butler Family Quilt, *shown on page 78. She presented the quilt to her husband's parents at a family reunion. She overheard his mother saying, "Just look what we started!" and made it a permanent part of the quilt label.*

Happy 50th Anniversary Quilt Label

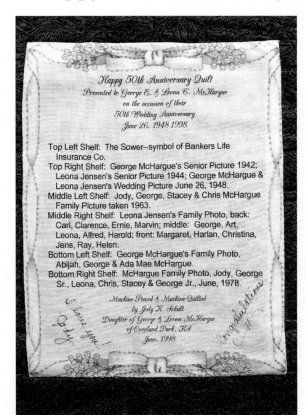

Jody Schult used her own computer to scan the photos and to print them directly onto fabric (see page 150). She also made a computer-generated quilt label that explained all the images on the quilt's front (see page 138).

Jody shaped her quilt as a bookshelf to make a unique wall hanging. Use your own imagination to create your family heirloom.

Resources

Computer Supplies
CompUSA Inc.
Over 200 computer superstores nationwide

CompUSA Net.com Inc.
Online computer superstore for Internet sales
www.compusanet.com

General Quilt Supplies
Contact the following companies
for a free catalog.

Connecting Threads
P.O. Box 8940
Vancouver, WA 98668-8940
1-800-574-6454

Hancock's of Paducah
3841 Hinkleville Road
Paducah, KY 42001
1-800-845-8723
fax (502) 443-2164
www.Hancocks-Paducah.com

Keepsake Quilting™
Route 25B, P.O. Box 1618
Centre Harbor, NH 03226
1-800-865-9458
www.keepsakequilting.com

The Quilt Farm
P.O. Box 7877
St. Paul, MN 55107
1-800-435-6201
www.quiltfarm.com

Photo Transfer
Photos-To-Fabric™
Mallery Press
4206 Sheraton Drive
Flint, MI 48532-3557
1-800-278-4824
www.quilt.com/amisimms

Rotary-cutting Rulers and Mats
Omnigrid, Inc.
1560 Port Drive
Burlington, WA 98233
1-360-757-4743

Rubber Stamps, Pigma™ Pens, Ink
Wallflower Designs
Susan McKelvey
P.O. Box 307
Royal Oak, MD 21662
Send $3.00 for catalog.

Template Material
Cut-Your-Own Templates
Flynn Quilt Frame Company
1000 Shiloh Overpass Road
Billings, MT 59106
1-800-745-3596
www.flynnquilt.com

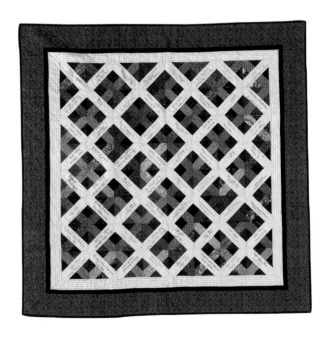